Winter Park Library

INTRODUCTION TO DEFENSIVE BIDDING

INTRODUCTION TO DEFENSIVE BIDDING

by Ronald P. Von der Porten

♠ ♡ ◇ ♣

PRENTICE-HALL, INC. ENGLEWOOD CLIFFS, N.J.

Introduction to Defensive Bidding
by Ronald P. Von der Porten

© 1967 by Prentice-Hall, Inc.

Copyright under International and Pan American
Copyright Conventions

Library of Congress Catalog Card Number: 67-25630

Printed in the United States of America
T

Prentice-Hall International, Inc., *London*
Prentice-Hall of Australia, Pty. Ltd., *Sydney*
Prentice-Hall of Canada, Ltd., *Toronto*
Prentice-Hall of India Private Ltd., *New Delhi*
Prentice-Hall of Japan, Inc., *Tokyo*

Foreword

Contract Bridge is a game with many facets. In order to become an adept player, you must learn how to bid the hand, how to play the hand, how to compete in bidding, and how to offer a good defense.

Most books on Contract Bridge are written for the novice or inexperienced player. Many attempts to cover all parts in a single volume often result in only skimming the surface.

The Series concept developed by Prentice-Hall is especially good for teaching one how to play Contract Bridge—this book is one of four volumes in the Introductory Series. Although they are intended for beginners, each book contains great value for the intermediate as well as the near-expert player.

The author is a young star in the Bridge firmament. At the age of 25 he rose to prominence as a team member representing North America in International competition, in 1962. Since that time, Ron Von der Porten has had many victories in top-flight competition and has earned his place in the all-time expert class.

Mr. Von der Porten, in cooperation with favorite partner Lewis L. Mathe, concentrated his attention on problems connected with defensive and competitive bidding. Consequently, he has developed an approach which, in some respects, is as new as today and he has succeeded in presenting a somewhat difficult subject in simple and understandable form.

ALVIN LANDY

Contents

	Foreword	v
1.	What Is Defensive Bidding?	1
2.	What Are Our Basic Weapons?	3
3.	The Takeout Double	7
	Quiz I	24
	Answers	25
4.	After the Takeout Double	29
	Quiz II	65
	Answers	66
5.	The Overcall	69
	Quiz III	82
	Answers	83
6.	After the Overcall	85
	Quiz IV	105
	Answers	106
7.	The Jump Overcall	109
	Quiz V	115
	Answers	115
8.	Notrump Overcalls	117
	Quiz VI	131
	Answers	132
9.	Preemptive Overcalls	135
	Quiz VII	141
	Answers	142
10.	The Direct Cue-Bid	143
	Quiz VIII	145
	Answers	145
	Index	149

1

What Is Defensive Bidding?

♠ ♡ ◊ ♣

A defensive bid is made after an opponent has opened the bidding. We shall be concerned here only with the partnership which has not opened the bidding. By competing effectively, this partnership can accomplish a number of goals:

(1) To determine safely and accurately the strength and suit distributions of the combined hands so as to be able to decide whether it would be better to defend against the opponents' contract or to play the hand themselves, even at the risk of a small penalty.

(2) To lay the groundwork for effective defensive play.

(3) To make it difficult for the opponents to exchange information and reach their best contract.

While it is true that there is an advantage to the side which makes the opening bid, we shall find that the competing pair has some weapons which are not available to the opening bidder. If partners will learn and conform to the principles set forth in the following chapters, they will be able to exchange information as accurately as the opponents who have opened the bidding.

2

What Are Our Basic Weapons?

♠ ♡ ◇ ♣

WEAPON NUMBER ONE:
THE TAKEOUT DOUBLE

Every time your opponents open the bidding, you are presented with an advantage. Your advantage is the opportunity to double, a call which is usually denied the opener's side except in rare, specific cases which may occur later in the auction. When you learned the scoring table, you found out how a player could be penalized by a double, but besides the penalty double there is also the takeout double. A takeout double consists of doubling over an opening bid or response in order to induce partner to bid his suit. This call is the single most useful tool of the competing side—and the most misused.

WEAPON NUMBER TWO:
THE OVERCALL

The opening bidder attempts to give a picture of his hand to his partner in as few bids as possible. He opens most hands with one of a suit, and he has begun to describe his hand by bidding his best suit or one of his best suits. You, as an opponent, can also begin describing a hand with one or two suits. You can use the call known as the *overcall* or, if you ever get around to reading a British text, the *overbid*. (In this country an overbid refers to bidding more than your hand warrants, and it usually results in an apology to partner.) An overcall consists of bidding a suit or notrump over an opening bid or response at the cheapest possible level. (Overcalls at a level other than the cheapest possible, such as opponent—1 ♡, you—2 ♠ or opponent—1 ♡, you—3 ♠, will be treated separately.)

WEAPON NUMBER THREE:
THE JUMP OVERCALL

You can show specific hands by the use of an overcall that is one level higher than is necessary (opponent—1 ♡, you—3 ♣).

Logically enough, a call of this nature is referred to as a *jump overcall.*

WEAPON NUMBER FOUR:
THE PREEMPTIVE OVERCALL

Other specific holdings can be shown by leaping to various high levels over an opponent's opening bid or response (opponent—1 ♡, you—3 ♠; or opponent—1 ♣, you—4 ♡; or opponent—1 ◇, partner—pass, opponent—1 ♡, you—4 ♣). These calls are referred to as *preemptive overcalls.*

WEAPON NUMBER FIVE:
THE UNUSUAL NOTRUMP

You can show specific two-suited hands by jumping to two notrump over an opening bid of one of a suit. This call is known as the *unusual notrump* and is a very valuable device when used properly. One player out of a thousand uses it properly. To the other nine hundred and ninety-nine it is less than useless.

WEAPON NUMBER SIX:
THE THREE-NOTRUMP OVERCALL

A leap to three notrump over an opening bid or response shows a certain hand pattern that contains a long, solid minor suit and a stopper in the suit or suits bid by the opponents.

WEAPON NUMBER SEVEN:
THE CUE-BID

A bid of the opener's suit directly over the opener (opponent—1 ♠, you—2 ♠) is referred to as a *cue-bid* and is forcing to game. It is the equivalent of an opening two bid.

That's your arsenal. You will notice that you have all the devices available to the opener, with the added options of the takeout double and the cue-bid; furthermore, you may use the information given to you by your opponent's opening bid. We shall now try to find out the most effective uses of the seven basic weapons and then see how we can mold them into an effective defense or offense.

3

The Takeout Double

♠ ♡ ◇ ♣

You are dealt:

♠ Q J 6 5   ♡ A Q 7 5   ◇ 5   ♣ A J 9 4

You are ready to open the bidding with one club, and the person to your right opens with one diamond. You know that you have a good hand and that your side could easily have a part score or even a game. The problem is finding the best place to play. The first step is for you to say "double"—the takeout double in its most classic form, showing an opening hand with support for all the unbid suits and shortness in the suit opened.

We have defined the takeout double as a double made over an opening bid or response in order to induce partner to bid his suit. By exchanging information in a series of bids following the takeout double, a partnership is able to find the best suit or no-trump contract at the correct level. Without getting involved in the very subtle nuances that are employed by the top experts, we shall attempt to trace the paths that are available from the double through the final bid. We shall also attempt to describe the patterns of hands which qualify for the takeout double and differentiate, both here and in later chapters, between the double and the various other bids available to the competing side.

THE DIRECT DOUBLE AT THE ONE LEVEL

The example used to begin this chapter is the most common situation in which the takeout double occurs, the doubler sitting directly behind, or "over," the opening bidder. When you make this call, you are describing a hand with at least the value of an opening bid—providing you are not a passed hand—and with a tolerance for the unbid suits. You are requesting that your partner name his best suit and show his overall strength.

Your right-hand opponent opens with one heart, and you hold the following hands:

(1) ♠ A Q 7 4   ♡ J 3   ◊ J 7 6 2   ♣ K Q 5
(2) ♠ K J 7   ♡ 5   ◊ A Q 9 8 7   ♣ K J 5 4
(3) ♠ A Q 4 3 2   ♡ 6 4   ◊ A J 3   ♣ A J 3

All of these hands constitute takeout doubles. They do not have the perfect 4-4-4-1 distribution which the opening example had, but they all are hands *with at least the value of an opening bid and a tolerance for the unbid suits*. If you find yourself in a position where the player at your right opens and your hand fits these requirements, your first thought should be to double rather than to bid a suit of your own. We are studying takeout doubles before overcalls so that you will acquire the valuable habit of doubling with a hand such as hand (3) above. Almost no aspect of bridge is more widely misunderstood than the principle involved in this example. By doubling, you describe a good hand —not only offensively, but defensively—while by overcalling, you will be describing a hand which is strong as an offensive weapon but which lacks defensive values and is suited primarily for play in the suit bid. The player who overcalls with hand (3) creates a false picture in his partner's mind concerning both the defensive potential and the possibility of playing in a suit other than spades. I suspect that most players know they are making the inferior call when they overcall, but there is the overwhelming desire in most players to wind up as the declarer, and a one-spade overcall is the quickest way. Remember, if you and your partner both get into the habit of making the best bid, you will each get to play your share of hands—you may even wind up stealing a few which the opponents should be playing.

The direct double at the one level may be used with hands which range in value from a minimum opening one bid to just short of an opening two bid. If your hand is in the minimum range, it must conform more to the requirements of tolerance for all the unbid suits and shortness in the opener's suit. *When doubling an opening bid in one major, you should have at least good three-card support for the other major.* Again, with a minimum double you should have maximum support for the other major. As you have more values, you can double without adhering quite so strictly to the requirements, since you will be able to describe your hand more clearly in subsequent bids. This luxury is not available when you are holding minimum values, because you have only one bid coming to you.

Your right-hand opponent opens with one spade, and you hold the following hands:

(1) ♠ 7 5	♡ 9 7 4	◇ A K 8 4	♣ A J 8 4
(2) ♠ 7 5 3	♡ A K 2	◇ A Q J 8 4	♣ A 5
(3) ♠ 8 7 4 2	♡ A Q 4	◇ A 7 4 3	♣ K 4
(4) ♠ 8 7 4 2	♡ A Q 4	◇ A K 4 2	♣ A 4

On hands (1) and (3) you should pass. On hand (1) you have minimum values, but your heart support—the other major —is inadequate. Add the club king, and you would double even with the bad heart holding, since you would then have additional values. You should not have minimum strength and minimum support for the other major on the same hand. Hand (3) should be passed because you have minimum strength, only three-card support for the other major, and too many cards in the opener's suit. You should have little desire to play the hand, but you would not mind if the opponents played it.

You should double with hands (2) and (4). In both cases you have too much strength to pass, even though you have holdings which are otherwise not ideal. On hand (2) you have only three hearts, and you hold three small cards in the suit opened, but you have sufficient strength to bid your diamonds if partner replies with two clubs. A double followed by a bid of a new suit shows a strong hand and a good five-card suit. We will cover these sequences later, but you should try to remember that if you plan to bid a suit of your own after you double, you will be describing a strong hand to your partner. You also suggest support for the unbid suits. Hand (4) is not an ideal double, because you hold too many spades, but you could easily miss a game if you pass. You should double and pass any non-jump responsc by partner. IIand (3) could casily cnd in a disaster at the two level after a double, but hand (4) is rich enough in high cards that you must risk a penalty in return for the chance of a game.

You may be in a position to make a takeout double after you have passed originally. Again, at this point we are dealing only with a double directly over the opening bidder. After three passes your right-hand opponent opens. You can double only with at least four-card support for the other major or at least eight cards in the majors if a minor was opened. Remember, you have passed originally, and the opponents will be alert to double you for penalties. Your values should be no more than two low cards in the suit opened and almost an opening bid.

In many cases you must gauge the pros and cons before deciding whether or not to enter the auction. The expert player comes in when he has much to gain and little to lose; the duffer does the opposite. At all levels of competition the winning player is the one whose judgment in competitive auctions is the keenest. Knowing when to make the immediate takeout double and when to pass is the first step.

THE TAKEOUT DOUBLE AFTER
BOTH OPPONENTS HAVE BID

The takeout double is not confined to the classic case of the person sitting directly over the opener. In our definition, we also mentioned that a double over a response could be a takeout double, and in most situations this is the case. Confusion develops as the auctions become more involved as to which doubles are for takeout and which are for penalties. Any low-level double which follows a response to an opening bid is for takeout *providing partner of the doubler has not entered the auction.*

SOUTH	WEST	NORTH	EAST
1 ♡	pass	2 ♡	double

This double would be for takeout.

SOUTH	WEST	NORTH	EAST
1 ♡	2 ♣	2 ♡	double

This double would be for penalties.

There is a limit to how high the auction can go before all doubles become primarily for penalties.

SOUTH	WEST	NORTH	EAST
1 ♠	pass	4 ♠	double

In this auction the doubler has a very good hand and probably very few spades, but partner should not take it out unless he has a long suit of his own. He would have to take out at the five level, which would mean he would be contracting for eleven tricks. Obviously it is more often wise to take a profit against four spades doubled.

If the opponents have bid two suits before you get a chance to act, your double would ask partner to name one of the other suits.

SOUTH	WEST	NORTH	EAST
1 ♢	pass	1 ♠	double

A double here would describe a hand with the value of an opening bid and at least four-four distribution in clubs and hearts. The more cards you hold in the suits, the less high-card strength is required. With only four-four in the unbid suits, you would need about fifteen points to enter the auction, especially if the auction has proceeded to the two level. Also, the higher the auction is when it gets to you, the better your hand should be to double. With

♠ K Q 8 4   ♡ A Q 8 3   ◇ J 7 4   ♣ 6 5

you would double over 1 ♣–pass–1 ◇, but would pass 1 ◇–
pass–2 ♣. The level of the auction, the length of your suits, the
high-card strength of your hand, and the vulnerability are the
factors which must be judged before a decision is reached about
whether or not to act. Remember, if the player at your left has
opened, the person at your right has gone to the two level, and
you are thinking of doubling, the chances are that your partner
has very few cards. You should come in only with good distribution in the unbid suits or with a very good hand in high cards
and *at least* four-four in the unbid suits. With a good hand and
length in their suits, let them go down.

There will be times when the bidding comes to you:

SOUTH	WEST	NORTH	EAST
1 ♡	pass	1 NT	?

You would double here just as if you were over the heart
bidder, except that your hand would not be an absolute minimum. The one level has been denied to you, and you have the
added information that your partner could not bid over one
heart.

THE DELAYED TAKEOUT DOUBLE

In certain auctions your hand will not be suited for any
action at your first opportunity, but because of the opponents'
bidding you will want to act at your second turn. You are dealt:

♠ K J 7 3   ♡ 5 4   ◇ A Q 10 5 4   ♣ 5 4

and the right-hand opponent opens with one heart. Even if you
are not vulnerable, your hand does not rate a double, because
of the lack of high cards and clubs. A diamond overcall is also
not recommended, so you should pass. The bidding now proceeds: one notrump to your left, pass by partner, and two clubs
by the opener. You would now double, and your partner would

assume that you have spades, diamonds and a hand not good
enough to have entered on the first round. You have described
your holding perfectly, since with a five-card spade suit of any
strength you would have bid the suit over one heart.

The delayed takeout double applies only when the bidding
of a second suit by the opponents transforms your holding from
a hand that was not biddable into one that is. How strong you
must be depends on the length of your suits, the vulnerability
and the strength of the opponents' bidding. You still hold

♠ K J 7 3   ♡ 5 4   ◊ A Q 10 5 4   ♣ 5 4

but now the bidding proceeds:

SOUTH	WEST	NORTH	EAST
1 ♡	pass	2 ♣	pass
2 ♡			

You would come in only if you were not vulnerable, since
your left-hand opponent has not limited his hand as in the original sequence.

The delayed takeout double is very valuable in setting up
saves against makeable games by the opponents. (A *save* is an
unrealistic contract which you reach in order to prevent opponents from playing the hand in a game contract which you are
fairly sure they can make. You "save" because your opponents
make fewer points from your undertricks than they would for
making their own contract. Furthermore, if they are vulnerable,
you prevent them from winning the rubber.) Since the bid shows
a hand with two suits, any hand where partner is weak but has
a five-card suit that fits is valuable as a cheap save. Partner
should be able to judge with accuracy at what level he feels the
opponents should be allowed to play the hand.

SOUTH	WEST	NORTH	EAST
1 ♡	pass	2 ♣	pass
2 ♡	double		

The partner of the doubler *knows* he can save in four spades with a hand like

♠ Q 10 7 6 3   ♡ 3   ◇ J 8 7 2   ♣ 6 3 2

He fits both suits and has no defensive values to defeat a heart contract.

One word of caution—confusion exists even in established partnerships over the meaning of the double in the following auction:

SOUTH	WEST	NORTH	EAST
1 ♠	pass	1 NT	pass
2 ♠	double		

This auction dictates that your double is for penalties. No new suit has been bid to transform the offensive value of your hand; you are sitting over the bidder; your left-hand opponent has shown limited values, and the opponents sound like they have a misfit. Your hand should be something like

♠ A Q 10 9 6   ♡ A   ◇ J 7 6 3   ♣ A 6 5

These things do happen, and it is nice to know you can double without your partner removing to three hearts. This auction also differs from the one that begins:

SOUTH	WEST	NORTH	EAST
1 ♠	pass	2 ♠	pass
pass			

If you were to double now, it would be a *balancing double* for takeout. We will cover the balancing double later, but you can see that this is a different case, because here the opponents are not showing a misfit but *are* showing weakness. You are in the "pass out" position (i.e., a pass by you will end the auction), and you must act or let the opponents play. At low levels you will often double in order to keep the bidding open and force the opponents to get to a higher contract which you hope to defeat.

THE DOUBLE OF A ONE-NOTRUMP OPENING BID

The double of one notrump differs from the double of other one-level openings. Since your opponent has not opened a suit, you are not given the advantage of being short in his suit. And since the notrump opener is showing a good hand, you are entering an auction where your partner is almost sure to have a weak hand. Your double, therefore, should have either a minimum of 16 points or a running suit with some entries. When you double one notrump, you are asking partner to pass, and you should have a hand which can defeat the contract. It is not a takeout double. You would double one notrump with any of the following hands:

(1) ♠ A Q 6   ♡ A K 7 4   ◊ A 8 7 4   ♣ 8 6
(2) ♠ Q J 10 9 5 3   ♡ A 2   ◊ A 2   ♣ Q J 5
(3) ♠ 6 2   ♡ K Q J 7 3 2   ◊ A Q 4   ♣ A 2

Your partner should not bid unless he has a very weak hand *and* a long suit. With a weak, evenly distributed hand he must pass.

TAKEOUT DOUBLES AT HIGHER LEVELS

The area covering the level at which a double changes from takeout to penalty is one of the haziest in bridge. There is much disagreement even among top experts.

Doubles of preemptive opening bids up to and including four diamonds are primarily for takeout, except doubles of four clubs and four diamonds in the "direct" position. (A double in the "direct" position is a double which is made by the player in the position directly behind, or over, the opener.)

The higher the bid which is opened, the better your hand

must be to double. There are other factors which must be considered before you decide whether or not to double, the most important of which is the vulnerability. If you are vulnerable and the opponents are not, you would need a very good hand, such as

♠ A Q 7 5   ♡ 5   ◊ A J 7 2   ♣ A J 4 3

to double an opening bid of three hearts. With the vulnerability reversed, you would double with as little as

♠ A J 7 2   ♡ 4   ◊ A J 6 4   ♣ K 8 3 2

Other factors to be considered are your length in the other major and also the number of passes before the preempt. If both your left-hand opponent and your partner have passed, you can double a little light, since both hands are limited and your partner is probably not broke. If, on the other hand, only your partner has passed, you should have solid values, since your partner may have nothing and the hand to your left may have all the outstanding cards. It will take a while before your judgment in these situations becomes accurate, but if you are alert to the above factors you should arrive at the correct solutions before too long. Again, we are discussing here only doubles which are directly over the bidder. Doubles after an auction such as 3 ♠—pass—pass will be discussed under the topic of *the balancing double*.

The higher the preempt, the more likely it is that your partner will pass your double. Any double directly over a preempt at the three level should be treated as almost exclusively for takeout. Doubles of four clubs and four diamonds in the direct position should be left in unless you have a five-card major or a very distributional hand with a four-card major and a long minor. It is better to take your profits—remember, the preempter has contracted to take ten tricks—than to attempt to slide into a fit in a major with only a four-card suit. When a person preempts with four of a minor, you can be reasonably sure that your four-four fit is going to run into a four-one or five-zero split between the opponents.

Doubles from four hearts up should be treated as primarily for penalties. Partner removes them at his own risk and only if he feels he can make what he bids with a minimum of trump support from the doubler. With

♠ K J 10 9 6 4   ♡ 8 7 3   ◊ 5   ♣ 6 5 3

you would bid four spades over any four-level double by your partner. You have limited defensive values and a suit that will play opposite any holding partner may have. You don't know that he has good spades, but you do know that he has a good hand.

You have several courses of action open to you when your right-hand opponent opens with a three bid. You can double, overcall, cue-bid his suit, jump overcall or bid three notrump. Most important, you can pass! Don't be rushed into the bidding just because the person at your right has announced weakness. If you bid, you are contracting for either nine or ten tricks on a hand where the suits will split badly. You must have your values in order for your partner to have confidence in your bidding. Shading your bids will work on the odd hand, but it will cost a fortune in the long run, because your partner will start bidding his hands incorrectly for fear that you are in the bidding on nothing. It is far better for each partner to bid his *own* hand accurately than for one to be an overbidder and his partner a "compensator."

We shall pursue the topic of bidding over preempts further in other chapters, but try to remember that direct doubles over any bid up through three spades are primarily for takeout; over any bid from four clubs on up, they are primarily for penalties.

THE BALANCING DOUBLE

A balancing double is a takeout double which is made by a player who is in the pass out position. Since the double is preceded by two passes, the player who balances—either by doubling or by overcalling in this position—is keeping the auction alive. Many thousands of pages have been written about the beauties of balancing and about how the balancer must do his tightrope act in order to "protect" his partner. The theories are that since the opponents are dying out at a low level, your partner must have a good hand, and that the less you have, the better partner's hand must be. The avid balancer will "protect" his partner with as little as six points at the one level. This "protection" will work out on hands where partner should, in the style we are trying to learn, have bid himself. In the cases where partner doesn't have a good hand, we merely give the opponents another chance to find their best suit and often propel them into a makeable game or even slam.

We have saved the balancing double for the end of this section on takeout doubles because we feel it is not nearly the cure-all it is made out to be. In fact, the balancing double on very weak hands should be made in only a very few auctions, and the auction that begins 1 ♣–pass–pass is definitely not one of them. The "balancers" say that because the opponents are showing weakness, partner must have a good hand, and we must "protect" him by bidding. If partner does have a good hand, it is in clubs, and a bid with no cards by us will serve no purpose other than getting the opponents out of their worst contract and into their best one, possibly at the game level. Partner has numerous weapons he could have employed over the one-club bid, and we are not going to insult him by telling him he didn't know what he was doing when he passed. In some styles, a direct overcall, such as 1 ♣–1 ♡, cannot be made without an opening bid, so that the person in the pass out position must indeed protect. As we shall see in the chapter on overcalling, we do not put such limitations on the overcaller, so that we do not need to protect a partner who has passed on his first turn.

We will treat the balancing double at the one level much the same as the direct double. You need not have a full opening bid, but if you don't, you should have close to it, and you should also have good holdings in the unbid major or majors.

SOUTH	WEST	NORTH	EAST
1 ◇	pass	pass	?

You would double here with a minimum of

♠ A J 7 3   ♡ Q 10 7   ◇ A 4   ♣ 9 8 6 4

You have enough defensive values against a major suit contract to make a game by the opponents unlikely. With any less than this we recommend a pass. There are other types of hands you will hold in the balancing position, and these will be discussed in the chapter on overcalls.

There are auctions where a balancing double may show considerably less than an opening bid. Auctions that consist of an opening one bid and a simple raise are often passed by the opening bidder.

SOUTH	WEST	NORTH	EAST
1 ◇	pass	2 ◇	pass
pass	?		

In an auction such as this you have already told your partner with your first pass that you couldn't act over a one-diamond opening. However, North then showed a weak hand with his diamond raise, and South limited his strength with his pass. Partner did pass two diamonds, but he may have a fair hand, because at the time he passed he had no idea about the strength of South's hand. He would have had to enter the auction at the two level, and although you know he doesn't have a powerhouse, he is surely not broke and could easily have the value of a minimum opening bid. You should make a balancing double with as little as

♠ K J 5 2   ♡ K 5 4 2   ◇ 5 4   ♣ Q 10 5

Partner will then make the decision as to how high he wants to push the opponents.

The main considerations when making a light balancing double are that you have already limited your hand with a previous pass and that the opponents have both bid their hands and are stopping *despite a fit*. If you are balancing when the opponents stop because of a misfit, you are going to go for a huge set.

SOUTH	WEST	NORTH	EAST
1 ♡	pass	2 ◊	pass
2 ♡	pass	3 ◊	pass
pass	double		

A double in this situation should never be for takeout. You might double with

♠ A Q 4   ♡ A Q 8 4 2   ◊ 4   ♣ K J 7 4

because the opponents have a probable misfit and your partner could have something in diamonds. Holding

♠ K J 6 4   ♡ 5 4   ◊ K 7 4   ♣ K 7 6 2

it might occur to you to make a balancing double not vulnerable, but your partner figures to have a weak hand with a long heart holding. When the opponents have announced a misfit, doubles in the balancing position are for penalties. In the above auctions any double after the three-diamond bid would be for penalties. Had you, as West, doubled on your second turn, it would have been a delayed takeout double for the other two suits.

In the rare situations where you will make a balancing double after passing at your first turn, you should make sure you have good support for the unbid major or majors. Your partner will be counting on it in his further actions.

In general, you should balance when the opponents have shown a fit and stopped; you should not balance when they have denied a fit and stopped. Balancing over a one-notrump response falls into the second category.

SOUTH	WEST	NORTH	EAST
1 ♡	pass	1 NT	pass
pass	double		

A double here would not be a balancing double; it would show a good hand with good hearts. You would want partner to pass unless he has a weak hand and a six-card suit. The same bid cannot be played both ways, so you cannot make this double as a balancing bid. This is fortunate, since you probably have a misfit anyway.

There are auctions which begin with a preempt followed by two passes. In these auctions the person in the pass out seat may double a shade lighter than in the direct position, since the partner of the preempter has passed. But only a shade, because partner has also passed and the partner of the preempter may have a fairly good hand.

SOUTH	WEST	NORTH	EAST
3 ♠	pass	pass	?

A double in this position is for takeout but is often passed. Partner may be sitting over the three-spade bidder with the remaining spades. All doubles of this nature through four diamonds should be for takeout. If you make a balancing double of four of a minor, you should have support for both majors. This differs from a double of four of a minor in the direct position, which *can* be made with the equivalent of an opening notrump.

In the balancing position you should double *only* with no values in the suit opened, since cards in that suit will be badly located. Again, the same call cannot be played two ways, so double a preempt in the balancing position only with shortness in the suit opened.

Doubles of four hearts or higher are better played for penalties, even in the balancing position. You should double with the equivalent of an opening notrump. If they make it, they were in game anyway.

In order to clear up the confusion that we have caused about doubles over preempts, let's summarize the action which your partner will take if you double.

In the direct position:

SOUTH	WEST	NORTH	EAST
3 ♣, 3 ◇, 3 ♡ or 3 ♠	double	pass	?

In these cases partner will play you for a good hand with shortness in the suit opened. He will take out your double unless he has good trumps.

SOUTH	WEST	NORTH	EAST
4 ♣ or 4 ♦	double	pass	?

In these auctions partner will play you for an opening notrump and will take you out with a reasonable five-card major and enough cards to give him a play for game. You may double with shortness in the opener's suit, but you must then have fast tricks to cash if partner leaves the double in.

SOUTH	WEST	NORTH	EAST
4 ♡, 4 ♠, 5 ♣ or 5 ♦	double	pass	?

Here partner will assume that you want to try to defeat the opening bid. He will leave the double in unless he has a very distributional hand.

In the balancing position:

SOUTH	WEST	NORTH	EAST
3 ♣, 3 ♦, 3 ♡, 3 ♠, 4 ♣ or 4 ♦	pass	pass	double

In all these cases, West will play you for shortness in the suit opened, good support for the unbid majors, and enough strength to make your bid reasonable according to the level and the vulnerability. West should take it out, but he can pass holding a poor hand and his values in the suit opened—

    ♠ 6 5   ♡ Q 5 4   ♦ J 6 5 2   ♣ 10 8 7 2

over a 4 ♣ or 4 ♦ opening or

♠ Q J 5 2   ♡ 6 3   ◊ J 7 3 2   ♣ 10 4 3

over a 3 ♠ opening. Over 3 ◊ he should take out to 3 ♠.

SOUTH	WEST	NORTH	EAST
4 ♡, 4 ♠, 5 ♣, 5 ◊	pass	pass	double

West will assume you have a good hand with good defensive values. He will bid only with a highly distributional hand. (With

♠ Q J 10 9 8 4   ♡ 5 4 3   ◊ 3   ♣ J 7 4

he would remove four hearts doubled to four spades.)

We have covered the balancing double and later will discuss the balancing overcall, but by the time you have finished the following quiz, you should be fairly adept at getting in and out of the auction at your first opportunity, thereby removing the need for your partner to "protect" you. The balancing theory will be minimized in your game. We feel that this style puts greater pressure on the opponents, with a maximum of accuracy and a minimum of danger. We cannot think of a more logical approach to competitive bidding.

Quiz I—Takeout Doubles

In taking these quizzes, we suggest you write down your answers. The answers follow directly, and it is difficult not to see several answers at once. Any problems you may have should be resolved by referring to the area in which the topic is covered. Don't proceed to the next chapter until you are sure you understand why we arrived at the conclusions we did.

Neither side is vulnerable; the player at your right deals and opens with one diamond. What action do you take with each of the following hands?

(1) ♠ A K 8 7 3	♡ A J 4	◇ 4 3	♣ A 6 3
(2) ♠ 2	♡ Q J 7 3	◇ A J 4	♣ A J 7 6 2
(3) ♠ A 7 6 2	♡ A 7 6 2	◇ 4	♣ K J 5 2
(4) ♠ 6 5	♡ Q 7 2	◇ A Q J 7 3	♣ A J 4
(5) ♠ A 10 9 8	♡ K J 4	◇ 7 6	♣ Q 9 8 7
(6) ♠ A Q J 10 7 3	♡ A Q 4	◇ 6	♣ A 7 2

Your left-hand opponent deals and opens with one heart, partner passes, and your right-hand opponent bids two hearts. With both sides vulnerable, what action do you take with each of the following hands?

(7) ♠ A 7 3	♡ Q 4	◇ K Q 7 3	♣ K 7 6 2
(8) ♠ A J 9 8	♡ 6	◇ A 7 6	♣ K 10 8 7 2
(9) ♠ K 8 7 2	♡ 6 2	◇ A J 5	♣ A 8 6 2
(10) ♠ A Q J 8 7	♡ 8	◇ A J 7 6	♣ A 5 2

No one is vulnerable. Three hearts is opened by the dealer to your right. How do you act with each of the following hands?

(11) ♠ A 8 7 2	♡ 5	◇ K J 5 4	♣ K J 5 4
(12) ♠ K 5	♡ Q 5	◇ A Q 7 6 2	♣ K J 7 4
(13) ♠ A Q J 5 4	♡ 4	◇ K J 5 4	♣ K J 3

(14) ♠ A J 4   ♡ 5 4   ◊ A Q J 4   ♣ K Q J 4
(15) ♠ A J 7 3   ♡ 5   ◊ A J 6   ♣ K J 6 4 2

Answers—Quiz 1

(1) Double   You will bid spades later, thereby describing a good hand with a good spade suit and support for the other suits.

(2) Pass   This is the perfect hand for a delayed double if the person at your left bids spades and no new suit is bid by the opener.

(3) Double   You have a minimum, but this is a good hand opposite any four-card fit in partner's hand.

(4) Pass   You have good defense and no offense.

(5) Pass   You may get a chance to make a balancing double if diamonds are raised. You are too weak to double directly.

(6) Double   You will then jump in spades to show an even better hand than number (1).

For discussion of (1) *through* (6), *see "The Direct Takeout Double."*

Hands (7) through (10) were tough, but hopefully they will suggest answers to two questions: Which hands shall we play and which shall we defend? What can we gain and what might we lose?

(7) Pass   This is a good hand in high cards but is better defensively than offensively. We don't hold four spades, the suit our partner will probably bid. With this many high cards, we can guess that the opponents probably have no game and that partner is probably very

broke. We have much to lose and little to gain from bidding.

(8) Double This is a far better double than the last hand. We may not be able to defeat four hearts, but may have a cheap save in four spades. We may even make it. No reason partner can't hold

♠ K Q 7 5 2   ♡ 7 5 3   ◇ 5 4   ♣ Q 6 5

or any of a thousand similar holdings. Here we have much to gain and almost nothing to lose if we double. Even if partner is broke and we go down, we are surely keeping the opponents from a makeable game.

(9) Pass We just don't have enough values of any kind to double. We hope partner can balance.

(10) Double We plan to bid spades at the three level and double if they get to game. They might make it, but we want to show a big hand and partner should be able to decide what to do. By doubling and then bidding spades, we are showing a good suit with tolerance for the other suits.

For discussion of (7) through (10) see "The Takeout Double After Both Opponents Have Bid."

(11) Pass You would double one heart, but you must have more in this situation. You would double if you were balancing, if there were two passes before the preempt, or if they were vulnerable, but if you bid in this case, partner would play you for a better hand and would surely bid more than you could make.

(12) Pass Don't double three hearts with only two spades. Bidding a minor has almost nothing to gain and plenty to lose if you run into a double.

(13)   Double   Perfect.
(14)   Double   Even with only three spades, we have to double. There is a very good chance we have a game and that partner can bid it with a reasonable spade suit. He might even be able to pass or bid three notrump.
(15)   Double   Another standard double, this one on the minimum side.

For discussion of (11) through (15), see "Takeout Doubles at Higher Levels."

4

After the Takeout Double

♠ ♡ ◇ ♣

This chapter will be more to your liking. You are going to learn how to respond to a takeout double by your partner, and if you learn well, you will wind up as declarer much of the time. So practice your dummy play and proceed.

The bidding comes to you:

SOUTH	WEST	NORTH	EAST
1 ◇	double	pass	?

This is a common auction. South and West have no less than opening bids; North has less than ten points (with ten or more he should have redoubled), and you are probably not looking at very much. *You must bid unless you hold at least five diamonds which will be good for three tricks,* as in the following hand:

♠ 6 5   ♡ 6 5   ◇ Q J 10 9 4   ♣ 7 6 4 2

Don't read on until the last thought has become law. If you pass your partner's takeout double just because you are very weak, you will have taken the first giant step toward the destruction of any kind of a partnership. Your partner realizes that you may be weak and that he has *forced* you to bid, so don't let him down. You have many bids available that show hands with some strength, so a minimum response by you will warn partner about the potential danger if he chooses to go on. Bid something! We shall soon see what.

The bidding proceeds:

SOUTH	WEST	NORTH	EAST
1 ◇	double	redouble	?

Again, South and West have no less than opening bids, but this time North has at least ten points for his redouble, and you are almost surely looking at a very weak hand. You can pass and let partner get himself off the hook, but if you have a decided preference for some suit, and especially if that suit is the cheapest one available, you should bid the suit. Your partner should not play you for any cards, only for a preference to play in the suit you bid.

With the same auction, you hold:

(1) ♠ 7 5 3   ♡ 7 5 3   ◇ 8 6 2   ♣ J 5 3 2
(2) ♠ 6   ♡ 10 5 4 3   ◇ J 10 9 8   ♣ 10 5 4 3
(3) ♠ 10 4 3 2   ♡ 6 5   ◇ 7 6 3   ♣ J 5 4 2

You should pass hand (1). You will be equally unhappy no matter which suit partner picks, and if he gets doubled, you will have avoided the "pleasure" of playing the hand.

Bid one heart with hand (2). If you pass, partner will almost surely bid spades, and you will have to rescue him at the two level. Remember, with his double he has shown some sort of heart support.

Pass with hand (3). Partner will probably bid hearts, but you can then correct to one spade if one heart is doubled. He knows that your spades aren't five long—if they were, you would have bid them immediately—so if you are in trouble, he may be able to bid two clubs and find the fit.

We have begun with these horrible hands as examples of what you may hold opposite a takeout double so that you will begin to understand two very important points:

(1) As the responder, you must be ready to bid some-

thing, no matter how weak your hand may be. You *must* bid when your right-hand opponent doesn't intervene, and you should be alert to bid even if he does.

(2)   As the doubler, you should be aware that you have *forced* your partner to bid, and if he makes a minimum response, you should not hang him for doing his duty. Bidding further with a minimum double would certainly be tantamount to hanging him.

A takeout double is made so that the partner of the doubler can name his suit. But he must also show his *strength*. By doing both of these things, the partnership can find the best contract at the best level. You may have a game in either a suit or no-trump against an opening bid. You may even have a slam. The following sections will show you how to get to the correct spot, as well as how to put on the brakes before you get into trouble if the correct spot is at the one level.

RESPONDING TO THE DIRECT TAKEOUT DOUBLE

The direct takeout double is far and away the most common beginning to auctions involving the takeout double. There are several paths open to the responder in answering his partner's request for him to bid. He must show not only his distribution, but also his strength or lack of strength. He may be able to respond by starting at the one level, but he must also know how to show his values when he is faced with assorted preemptive bids by his right-hand opponent.

The bidding goes:

SOUTH	WEST	NORTH	EAST
1 ♡	double	pass	?

As we have seen, East must bid unless his values are entirely in hearts, or unless they are such that he knows that one heart doubled will yield a fine profit, as would be the case with

♠ 5   ♡ K J 10 8 7   ◇ 7 6 4   ♣ 7 6 4 2

or with

    ♠ 5 4   ♡ K Q J 10 8   ◇ A 5 4   ♣ K 4 3

In most cases East will have a fairly poor hand, and he should show it by bidding any suit at the lowest possible level. In the case where the opening bid is one heart, a response of one spade, two clubs or two diamonds would show a hand of from zero to eight points and a preference for the suit bid. With very bad hands you should try to bid the other major if at all possible, since that is the suit for which your partner almost surely has good support, and since you are usually keeping the bidding at the lowest possible level. (The exception would be if partner's double is over one spade.)

After the heart opening, a double by partner and a pass to your right, you are faced with the following hands:

(1) ♠ 7 6 4 2   ♡ 7 5 4 2   ◇ Q J 7 2   ♣ 6 2
(2) ♠ J 4 2   ♡ 7 6 4 2   ◇ Q 5 3   ♣ Q 5 3
(3) ♠ Q 5 3 2   ♡ 7 6   ◇ 7 6   ♣ K Q 10 5 3

On hands (1) and (2) you should bid one spade. On hand (1) your diamonds are better than your spades, but you have a bad hand and should find a fit in spades at the lower level. A bid of two diamonds implies a five-card suit because it is the suit furthest from hearts, and the fact that you didn't bid a cheaper suit would seem to indicate the lack of one. With more than one four-card suit, you should bid the cheapest one first unless you plan to make another bid, and even then you should bid a major ahead of a minor. On hand (2) you must bid, and one spade is the least of evils.

On hand (3) you should bid two clubs with the intention of bidding spades next. You have just short of a jump response.

With the auction the same, you hold:

(4) ♠ 5 3   ♡ 7 6 2   ◇ Q J 7 6   ♣ K Q 7 6
(5) ♠ Q J 5   ♡ 9 8 3   ◇ 10 9 5 3   ♣ J 5 2
(6) ♠ Q 9 5 3 ♡ 6 2   ◇ Q 9 5 3 2 ♣ 6 2

Hand (4) rates two bids if the bidding doesn't get too high. Bid two diamonds with the intention of bidding three clubs next. With the same distribution and fewer high cards, you would bid two clubs and pass thereafter.

Hand (5) should respond with one spade. You have bad distribution and a bad hand. Bid the major and keep the bidding as low as possible.

You should bid one spade on hand (6) also. Your partner is almost sure to have support for the spades. You will make only one bid unless partner shows great strength.

So the things to remember when forced to make a response with a bad hand are these:

(1) You must bid unless you have long, strong trumps.

(2) Bid a new suit at the cheapest possible level (one no-trump is reserved for better hands).

    (a) You should usually bid the longest suit. However, if you have a reasonable major, if you are planning to make just one bid, and if the major is a cheaper bid than the minor, bid the major even if it is one card shorter than the minor. (See hands (5) and (6). Had the opening been one club, you would have bid one diamond.)

    (b) With suits of equal length, bid a major before a minor. With equal-length majors or equal-length minors, bid the cheaper if you plan to make only one bid, or the higher if you plan to bid both suits.

    (c) If you have no four-card or longer suit other than the opener's, bid your cheapest three-card suit.

If the player to your right puts in a bid, you should still bid if you have any reasonable suit. You can pass to show a bad hand, but a minimum bid does not show any great amount of strength. You would be indicating from five to nine points with at least a good four-card major or a fair five-card minor.

SOUTH	WEST	NORTH	EAST
1 ◊	double	1 ♡	?

Sitting East, you hold:

(1) ♠ K Q 10 5   ♡ 5 3   ◊ 7 6 2   ♣ J 5 4 2
(2) ♠ 10 5 4 3   ♡ 5 4 2   ◊ 5 4 2   ♣ A 4 3
(3) ♠ J 3 2   ♡ 7 3   ◊ 5 4 2   ♣ K Q 9 8 3

You should bid on hands (1) and (3) and pass hand (2). Hand (1) is a one-spade bid, and hand (3) rates a two-club call. If you don't bid now, the opener may raise hearts and you will be forced to make a decision at some higher level. By bidding, your partner will be in a position to make an intelligent decision if the opener goes higher in hearts. It is better to get into the auction early, if you have your values, than to wait and guess at a higher level when the opponents have already exchanged their information. Pass hand (2), because you don't have enough to bid unless you are forced to.

If the person at your right has bid to a higher level or raised his partner's suit to the two or three level, you should still attempt to find a bid when you have a good suit and don't have to go too high. If the level is one, two or three, your partner will consider your bid competitive as long as you don't jump. He should not get excited unless he holds a very strong double.

SOUTH	WEST	NORTH	EAST
1 ♡	double	2 ♡	?

Sitting East, you hold:

(1) ♠ K 10 7 3 2   ♡ 6 5   ◊ Q 5 3   ♣ J 4 2
(2) ♠ K J 10 4   ♡ 6 5   ◊ A 6 3   ♣ 10 5 4 2
(3) ♠ 5 3   ♡ 5 3   ◊ 5 3 2   ♣ A J 7 6 3 2

All these hands should be bid. If you don't bid now, either you will wind up selling out to two hearts, or you will find yourself faced with a nasty decision at a higher level. Hands (1) and (2) are two-spade bids, and hand (3) is a three-club bid. These are merely competitive bids, and *with better hands you must find bigger bids*. We will soon find out what these bids may be, but you must realize that bids in these situations do not show powerful hands, even though you are not required to bid. A pass would show a weak hand. A bid merely shows an interest not to be shut out of the bidding. You should not bid every time you have seven or eight points, but only when you have some reason to want to play the hand.

(4) ♠ K 5 3   ♡ Q J 4   ◇ Q 5 4 2   ♣ 5 4 2
(5) ♠ J 5   ♡ J 9 4 2   ◇ A 5 4 2   ♣ Q 5 4 2
(6) ♠ Q 4 2   ♡ J 5 3   ◇ K 4 2   ♣ Q 10 5 2

With the auction the same, you should pass with these hands. You have good defensive values but questionable offensive values. Experience will show you that these are the hands with which no one can make much of anything. And even if you can make a part score, how are you going to find out which one?

If your right-hand opponent redoubles, you should bid to keep your partner from rescuing to a suit higher than the one you hold. We covered this in the beginning of the chapter. You should also bid if you have a hand with some values. Not only should you bid, but you should rebid if the bidding stays at a low level. Your first bid might have been just a preference to play your suit; the second bid would show a fair hand. With a hand of nine points or more, you would jump or bid notrump.

Sitting East, you hold:

(1) ♠ K 10 7 3 2   ♡ 6 5   ◇ Q 5 3   ♣ J 4 2
(2) ♠ 7 3   ♡ 6 5   ◇ A J 7 6 3 2   ♣ 5 3 2
(3) ♠ 7 3   ♡ 6 5   ◇ 6 3 2   ♣ A J 7 6 3 2

The bidding proceeds:

SOUTH	WEST	NORTH	EAST
1 ♡	double	redouble	?

On hand (1) you would bid and rebid spades. Your first bid might have been a rescue. You are just a shade light to jump to two spades immediately.

Hand (2) rates only one bid, an immediate two-diamond bid. You must have some values to make this bid, because if you were very weak, you would pass and then rescue your partner at your next turn if he ran into a double. When you can rescue later at the cheapest level, you should bid originally only when you have a hand at least as good as this.

Hand (3) is worth two bids as long as the level remains at three. Your first bid might have been made to keep partner from bidding diamonds, so you must show a fair hand if possible.

The difference between hands (2) and (3) is rather obscure. The hands are included here not to confuse you, but to point out the kind of thinking that is required in order for a partnership to bid intelligently. Bridge is full of these little problems. They can make the game frustrating, but they are also what make it so interesting.

Sitting East, you are dealt:

(1) ♠ J 5	♡ K 9 8 6	◇ A 4 3	♣ 10 9 7 3
(2) ♠ 3	♡ J 10 9 7 6	◇ J 9 3	♣ 9 8 6 2
(3) ♠ Q 9 7 3	♡ K J 5 3	◇ 4	♣ A 7 3 2

Here is the auction:

SOUTH	WEST	NORTH	EAST
1 ◇	double	1 ♡	?

You were about to bid one heart yourself. There are times when the player at your right bids your suit in order to confuse your bidding. He may have a good diamond fit and be trying to keep your side from reaching a good heart contract. If you have a hand of more than seven points, and if your heart suit is no less than Q 10 7 2, you should double in order to tell partner that you have hearts and a fair hand.

Double one heart on hand (1). North took your bid, and with your partner's double this could easily be your hand. Double best describes your hand.

Pass hand (2). You do not want to encourage partner. If

he bids spades, you would run to hearts. He has guaranteed support with his double, and by not bidding until your second turn, you would describe a hand with long hearts but not enough values to double one heart.

Double hand (3). This is a very suspicious auction. Partner's double implies that he is short in diamonds, and you have a singleton. North almost surely has diamonds and is fooling around with his heart bid. You should double and later either cue-bid diamonds or jump in spades. In this way you will get to the best major-suit contract.

We have seen how to respond to the direct takeout double when holding bad hands. You will often hold these hands, and by bidding them correctly, you will be able to stop before disaster strikes. It is essential that the doubler recognize the danger signals which a minimum response may represent. We shall see later how the doubler should act when it is his turn to rebid, but at this stage it is important that the doubler realize that he has forced his partner to bid and that if the response is in the minimum range, he must be prepared to find the responder with a very poor hand. He must put himself in the responder's seat and then apply the golden rule.

Just as it is the doubler's responsibility not to get the partnership too high, it is often the responder's responsibility to get it high enough. With more than a minimum holding, the responder must make more than a minimum bid. He may never get the chance to bid again.

SOUTH	WEST	NORTH	EAST
1 ♡	double	pass	?

You, East, hold:

(1) ♠ K 10 5 4 2   ♡ 7 4 2   ◇ K 3 2   ♣ Q J
(2) ♠ 6 5   ♡ Q 10 7 4   ◇ K Q 3 2   ♣ 9 7 2
(3) ♠ 6 5   ♡ K J 9   ◇ K Q 3 2   ♣ Q 9 4 2
(4) ♠ J 5 4 2   ♡ J 7 2   ◇ K Q 10   ♣ A Q J
(5) ♠ K 10 9 8 6 2   ♡ 4   ◇ Q 7 6 3 2   ♣ 4

Bidding a suit at the minimum level will cause you to miss a game on four of the five hands. Partner, who has read the last section carefully, realizes that you may be very weak and that you will pass with any hand resembling

♠ A Q 7 3   ♡ 6 5   ◊ A J 4   ♣ K 10 8 5

Unless the opponents are very kind, you will wind up playing the hand in whatever minimum bid you make.

It is not enough to show your suit. *You must also show your strength.*

Hand (1) is a two-spade bid.
Hand (2) is a one-notrump bid.
Hand (3) is a two-notrump bid.
Hand (4) is a two-heart bid. (A cue-bid.)
Hand (5) is a four-spade bid.

These hands represent the various calls the responder can make to show hands with more than minimum values. He may also jump to three notrump on a hand a little better than number (3). *Only the cue-bid is forcing.* The other bids have specific limits. These limits are just as specific as those for a one-notrump opening bid. They must be adhered to just as strictly.

The Jump Response

This call shows values anywhere from a good nine to a bad twelve points. You should have a decided preference to play in the suit in which you jump, but you may jump on a good four-card major. When partner doubled, he promised major-suit support, so you should jump in a good four-card major rather than bid a minor. With both majors you would use a cue-bid, providing the opening bid was a minor. The jump response is not forcing, but by using it, you limit your hand and allow partner to decide whether or not he should go on.

SOUTH	WEST	NORTH	EAST
1 ♣	double	pass	?

Sitting East, you are looking at:

(1) ♠ K J 8 7 2   ♡ 8 7   ◇ K 7 6 2   ♣ 7 2
(2) ♠ A Q J 4   ♡ 8 7   ◇ Q 8 7 4 2   ♣ 7 2
(3) ♠ K 4 3 2   ♡ 4   ◇ K Q J   ♣ Q 7 6 4 2
(4) ♠ A Q 6 2   ♡ K 10 6 2   ◇ J 4 2   ♣ 7 6

Hands (1), (2) and (3) are two-spade bids. They all fall within the nine to twelve point limits, and they all have a decided preference for the suit bid. Notice that hand (3) contains a "bad" twelve or thirteen points. Your singleton is in a suit your partner has, but still must be counted for some value. If your clubs and hearts were reversed, you would cue-bid and carry on to game in whichever major partner showed a fit. Your hand would then exceed the upper limits for a jump response. Hand (1) may look meager, but if you match it up with any hand above a minimum double, you will see that game is very likely. Remember, with a minimum double your partner is not going to go on unless he fits your suit very well. *Your bid is limited, and the doubler should pass with a flat minimum double.*

Hand (4) falls within the range of a jump response, but it is not clear in which suit you should jump. Bid two clubs, and then raise partner's suit if he bids a major. We have not yet examined cue-bids, but this example is intended to show that the values for a cue-bid sometimes overlap the values for some other calls. You must learn to decide which action is the most descriptive.

Don't hesitate to jump on hands like number (1). You may get to some thin games, but many will make. You have a fit, and most important, you know where the outstanding cards are. You will know how to play the hand, and the finesses should work, because your partner's cards are over the opening bidder's. If you don't jump and as a result you begin to miss some good games, partner will feel he has to make more bids than he actually has coming. Then when you really are very poor, you will receipt for a large penalty. Bid your values, and partner will not feel compelled to bid them for you.

The One-Notrump Response

The one-notrump response to a takeout double is included in this section because this call is used to show hands with some limited values. It should not be made with less than six high-card points and a stopper in the suit opened. The upper limit is a bad ten points. The bid tends to deny a four-card major and does not necessarily show stoppers in any suit other than the one opened. Even if the right-hand opponent intervenes with one of a suit, a one-notrump bid by you does not guarantee a stopper in that suit. Partner has shown support for the overcalled suit when he doubled, but he has denied holding the suit opened.

SOUTH	WEST	NORTH	EAST
1 ♦	double	pass	?

As East, you hold:

(1) ♠ 6 5	♥ 7 6 3	♦ K 10 6 3	♣ K 4 3 2
(2) ♠ 6 5	♥ 7 6 3	♦ K Q 10 3	♣ K J 3 2
(3) ♠ J 7 6 5	♥ 6 3	♦ K 10 6 3	♣ Q 6 3
(4) ♠ 6 5 3	♥ J 6 2	♦ J 10 9 8	♣ Q 3 2

Bid one notrump on hands (1) and (2). On hand (2) you would bid a notrump even if North had intervened, but on hand (1) you would pass. To bid in this situation implies a maximum holding. However, you still cannot hold more than a bad ten points. On neither of these hands would you consider passing one diamond doubled. Your trumps are not good enough.

Bid one spade on hand (3). It is very close as to whether you should bid one notrump or one spade, but it is generally better to mention your major.

Hand (4) is a one-heart bid. You don't have enough to bid one notrump, and your trumps are not long or strong enough to pass.

The Two-Notrump and Three-Notrump Responses

Both of these responses are made with beefed up versions of the one-notrump response. Two notrump would be a good ten to a bad twelve, and three notrump would be a good twelve to about fifteen. With more you would cue-bid first in order to make sure that you are not missing a slam. If partner makes more than a minimum rebid, you would investigate further. These auctions will be covered more fully when we discuss cue-bids.

When you bid either two or three notrump, you should not have a good four-card major other than the one opened. You would either jump in the suit or, more likely, cue-bid.

These bids do not promise stoppers in all the unbid suits. The doubler has shown strength in the unbid suits, so the no-trump bidder's responsibility is to have stoppers in the suit opened and a hand which is suited for play in notrump.

A three-notrump bid will often be made on a hand with a long, semi-solid minor suit and stoppers in the opener's suit. When responding to a takeout double, you should think of bid-ding some number of notrump when you have cards in the opener's suit, limited length and strength in the unbid major or majors, and length and strength in the unbid minor or minors.

SOUTH	WEST	NORTH	EAST
1 ◇	double	Pass	?

You are East and hold:

(1) ♠ 6 5	♡ Q 6 2	◇ K J 2	♣ K Q 7 6 3
(2) ♠ 6 5	♡ 8 4 3	◇ A Q	♣ K Q J 7 6 3
(3) ♠ 6 5 2	♡ J 6 3 2	◇ K Q J 3	♣ A 2
(4) ♠ 6 5 2	♡ K Q J 2	◇ Q 9 3 2	♣ K 4

Hand (1) fits the requirements for a two-notrump response perfectly. Were you to bid three clubs, partner might pass when three notrump was on. Partner would never dream that you had two potential diamond stoppers if you failed to bid notrump or to make a cue-bid.

Bid three notrump on hand (2). A cue-bid would just confuse partner when he tries to find your major. Partner has an opening bid with support for the unbid suits. Keep writing down possible doubles, and you will see that almost invariably three notrump will be the best contract. If partner has a very big hand, he may even put you in six. Remember, three clubs is limited and not forcing, and partner may very likely pass. Only the idle rich can afford to bid three clubs with hands of this sort. If you have doubled with

♠ Q J 2   ♡ A Q 7 6 2   ◇ 4 2   ♣ A 8 2

you should pass a three-club bid. You *must* pass the three-no-trump response. Had partner been interested in your broken five-card heart suit, he would have cue-bid two diamonds. When partner responded three notrump, he said that he had heard your double and that he felt he could make three notrump. Don't insult him by bidding four hearts.

Two notrump is best on hand (3). You have a four-card major, but it is very anemic. Most of your cards are in the suit opened, and the hand falls squarely into the two-notrump range.

You would cue-bid two diamonds on hand (4). If partner bids hearts, you would put him in game, but if partner bids a black suit, you would bid the minimum number of notrump. In the latter case, partner will realize that you have a tolerance for notrump but also a tolerance for suit play.

The Cue-Bid Response

This bid—a bid of opener's suit after a takeout double—is misunderstood by most bridge players. It is avoided by most players because they do not realize its versatility. The average player has a vague feeling that the cue-bid must show a very big hand, and although he is aware that the expert uses the call somewhat more often than he, he is not at all familiar with the more common cases where the occasions to use the bid arise.

We have touched on several of them already. We shall now try to explain some of the more common sequences and show why the cue-bid is the only logical answer to many hands.

Before we begin, there are a few general rules which should be followed when contemplating cue-bidding the opponents' suit in response to a takeout double.

(1)   Make it a point not to cue-bid with less than nine points.

(2)   The cue-bid should be made only on hands where no other bid will describe your holding clearly. The other responses have certain limits, while the cue-bid is unlimited. If you can describe your hand with a limited bid, do so.

(3)   Any new suit you bid after you cue-bid is forcing. If you have a suit which you want to mention and your hand lacks the value of an opening bid, don't cue-bid. You will be getting the partnership to too high a level without knowing where you are headed. With less than an opening bid, you should use the cue-bid only on hands where you can either support whatever your partner bids or retreat to notrump.

SOUTH	WEST	NORTH	EAST
1 ♣	double	pass	?

You should respond with two clubs on each of the following hands:

(1) ♠ K 7 3 2   ♡ K 7 3 2   ◇ J 8 6 4   ♣ 4
(2) ♠ 6 5 4 2   ♡ A K 5 3   ◇ A 4 2   ♣ 6 2
(3) ♠ A Q J 4 2   ♡ Q 6 3   ◇ 6 5   ♣ A J 6
(4) ♠ A K J 3 2   ♡ A 3 2   ◇ K J 3 2   ♣ 2

Hand (1) is an absolute minimum. With any less you would bid one spade and later bid two hearts if you got the chance. With the same distribution and less than five points, you would bid one diamond and then stay out later. The cue-bid is made because you have good values over a takeout double and you do not know which suit to bid. If partner makes a two-level reply, you will pass. The doubler should show additional values if he has them. He can repeat the cue-bid with a good hand and no five-card suit, or he can jump in his five-card suit. If his hand were

♠ A Q 5 3   ♡ A 6 5   ♢ A Q 3 2   ♣ 3 2

the bidding would be as follows:

SOUTH	WEST	NORTH	EAST
1 ♣	double	pass	2 ♣
pass	3 ♣	pass	3 ♢
pass	3 ♠	pass	4 ♠
pass	pass	pass	

West doubles for takeout. East cue-bids with a minimum. West has additional values, which he shows by repeating the cue-bid. He has no suit in which to jump. (Had the doubler had a minimum, he would have bid his lowest four-card suit.) East bids his lowest four-card suit. West now shows a four-card spade suit, and East, who also has four spades, puts his partner in game. Without the use of the cue-bid, East might have selected spades anyway, but he might just as well have found West with four hearts and only three spades.

Hand (2) you will push to game. If partner replies with a major, you will put him in four. If he says two diamonds, you will repeat the cue-bid. Partner should not assume that this now shows a club suit. No one has placed clubs in your hand between the time you cue-bid two clubs and the next club bid.

If partner repeats his diamonds, you will assume he has no four-card major. Only with this sequence would you stop short of game. Partner should have something like

♠ A K 3   ♡ Q 7 2   ♢ K Q 8 7 3   ♣ 4 3

Hand (3) is a two-club bid because your only problem is finding the correct game or slam. If partner replies two diamonds, you can bid two spades. *Any new suit by the cue-bidder after a cue-bid is forcing.* If partner raises spades, you would go to four. If he bids a red suit, you would try three notrump. Had your partner been dealt

♠ K 6   ♡ A K J 10 2   ◊ A 7 4 2   ♣ 5 4

the bidding would proceed:

SOUTH	WEST	NORTH	EAST
1 ♣	double	pass	2 ♣
pass	3 ♡	pass	3 ♠
pass	4 ◊	pass	4 NT
pass	5 ♡	pass	6 ♡
pass	pass	pass	

After West jumps to three hearts in order to show additional values, East bids his spades in order to find the best suit. West bids four diamonds, and East goes to six hearts after making sure that West has at least one ace. East has taken charge, because he knows the value of West's hand.

Hand (4) will almost surely produce a slam. On hand (3) you needed a strong response in order to think in terms of six, but here any double should give you a good play. Rather than launch directly into Blackwood and go to six spades, you should start with a two-club bid. If South was psyching his opening bid, partner might even reply with something like three diamonds. In any case, diamonds may be the best slam, whether at the six or seven level. There is no sense in taking charge of an auction as long as partner has not yet limited his hand.

When your right-hand opponent bids a new suit after a takeout double by partner, you should use the last named suit for your cue-bid.

SOUTH	WEST	NORTH	EAST
1 ♣	double	1 ♡	2 ♡

Two hearts by East is a cue-bid. If he had a good heart suit, he would have doubled hearts.

Do not go out of your way to use cue-bids and repeated cue-bids in a strange game. As we have mentioned previously, most players are unfamiliar with the many uses of the bid and will only be confused. Cue-bids are the core of many of the disaster stories in the game's colorful history. Almost every top expert has had to learn the hard way about the indiscriminate use of this call. The fortunate ones were simply left in their cue-bids; the unluckier ones were left in doubled and redoubled cue-bids.

SOUTH	WEST	NORTH	EAST
1 ♣	double	pass	2 ♣
double	2 ♦	pass	3 ♣
double	pass	pass	redouble
pass	pass(!)	pass	

East was attempting to convey to West that he held two four-card majors and a good hand. West had heard of cue-bids, so he responded—once. South wanted to make sure he got a club lead, so he doubled when East cue-bid. North was shrewd enough to realize that South's doubles showed good clubs. South was delighted to lead trumps himself. Down 3,400—but don't waste too much sympathy on East. He should have been aware of West's limitations and should not have given him the chance to make the final, fatal decision. You must be sensitive to the strengths and weaknesses of your partners.

Cue-bids are extremely useful if used correctly. Work them out with your favorite partner, but use them with caution and only in the most obvious situations with unfamiliar partners. With very weak partners, try to avoid the use of the cue-bid. You may as well play the hand yourself—and not in the opponents' suit.

The Jump Response to Higher Levels

We have saved these responses for last because we feel that many players use them too often. Jumps to game in a major are often made on hands which could be bid more accurately with an initial cue-bid. While it is perfectly true that it is often better to make a direct bid and deny the opponents information to which they are not entitled, it is also true that getting to the best contract will get the money in the long run.

SOUTH	WEST	NORTH	EAST
1 ♣	double	pass	?

Holding

♠ A J 6 5 2	♡ A 6 2	◊ K 4 2	♣ 6 3

many players would bid four spades directly. In this case it is far better to cue-bid. Hearts could easily be the best contract. Jumps to game should be made on hands with which you are sure you are bidding the correct suit, and with which, by bidding to a high level, you may be preempting the opponents. On the above example, there is no question as to whose hand it is. Take your time and explore to find the best contract. Partner's spade support might not be too good, making a spade game difficult. Or—more likely—your partner may have a hand good enough to produce a slam. Also, if the opening bidder bids five clubs over your jump to four spades, your partner will have no idea about the defensive values you hold; he could, with good spade support, bid five spades. You would miss a good penalty and might not make five spades. Correct decisions can be made only if the bidding preceding the decision is accurate. Making the wrong choices in these situations is as disastrous as missing sure games.

If you jump to game, you should have a hand with limited defensive values and with a suit that will play opposite as little as a doubleton honor. The bid is somewhat preemptive, so partner will not try for a slam unless he holds a good hand *with controls*. A lot of high-card points in kings, queens, and jacks are not enough. The doubler must have aces to go on.

SOUTH	WEST	NORTH	EAST
1 ♣	double	pass	?

You are East and hold:

(1) ♠ Q J 10 9 6 3 2   ♡ 2   ◇ Q J 6 3   ♣ 2
(2) ♠ A Q J 10 3   ♡ 4 3   ◇ J 7 6 3 2 ♣ 4
(3) ♠ 4   ♡ Q J 10 9 7 6 3 ◇ J 3 2   ♣ 4 2
(4) ♠ K Q J 4 2   ♡ J 5 3 2   ◇ A   ♣ Q 6 3

Hands (1) and (2) are four-spade bids. You should have
a reasonable play, your defensive values are limited, and you
know that spades will offer the best play for game.

Bid three hearts on hand (3). A double jump short of game
is best played to show a long suit with no defense. Partner will
go to game with controls.

Hand (4) is best handled with a cue-bid. If partner bids
a red suit, you would then mention spades. You would wind up
in four spades if partner never bids hearts.

RESPONDING TO DOUBLES OF PREEMPTS

At the end of Chapter Three, we summarized the actions
that the responder would take over doubles of preempts. We
discussed whether or not the responder should take the double
out. But it is not enough to know when you should bid—you
must also know *how much* to bid.

Preempts, when properly used, make things difficult for the
opponents. That is why we will learn to bid the limit of our hand
in as few bids as possible when overcalling, jump overcalling or
preemptively jump overcalling. The opponents, however, are also
entitled to preempt, and we shall have to deal with them as best
we can. You will not always find your best contract after a preempt, but you should be able to find reasonable bids and avoid
too many disasters. And a disaster is not only bidding too much,
but also bidding too little and missing easily makeable games.

Responding to Three-Level Doubles

Don't be shy!
This is a situation where you should bid a lot on hands

that you would have been glad to trade in when they were dealt. The required strength of your partner's double varies according to who has passed and who is vulnerable, but in all cases he must have a good hand. He is requesting you to bid at least at the three level, so if you have any kind of a hand, and especially if you have any kind of a suit, you should make more than a minimum bid.

In order to pass, you do not need the fantastic trump holdings that you needed to leave in a double at the one level, but you should have at least one trump trick and a hand with no other clear action. Pass with weak hands *only* if you have good trumps.

The cue-bid is sometimes used to show interest in both majors if three of a minor has been opened. The doubler should not get excited unless he has a fantastic hand. The cue-bidder may bid four clubs over three clubs doubled with as little as

♠ K 7 6 2   ♡ A 7 6 2   ◇ 4   ♣ 8 7 4 2

This hand should play well opposite the doubler's better major. Bidding game is a better gamble than guessing which suit to bid at the three level and then playing short of game.

In many cases you will be forced to jump to game with anemic suits. You may not have the room to cue-bid, and you may be short in the other major. With

♠ 5 4   ♡ K J 3 2   ◇ K 7 6 2   ♣ A 4 3

you would jump to four hearts over three clubs doubled. Three notrump could be right, but you have only one chance to bid, and four hearts seems to be the better game. You could pass three clubs doubled, but you won't beat them by much, and four hearts should have a very good play. This is the type of decision that is often encountered after a preempt. Don't underbid and force your partner to worry that you can't bid your values in these sequences. There is nothing more expensive than a partner who feels he has to bid again with just a normal takeout double.

SOUTH	WEST	NORTH	EAST
3 ♣	double	pass	3 ♡
pass	4 ♡	double	pass
pass	pass		

NORTH
♠ A Q 7 5 2
♡ A J 4
◇ K 7 6
♣ 5 2

WEST
♠ K J 8 4
♡ K Q 8 5
◇ A Q J 10
♣ 9

EAST
♠ 10 9 3
♡ 10 9 3 2
◇ 9 8 3
♣ K 10 4

SOUTH
♠ 6
♡ 7 6
◇ 5 4 2
♣ A Q J 8 7 6 3

You will avoid these disasters if you bid three hearts in the East position only when holding a bad hand. Partner will soon realize that if you had had much more, you would have bid more. He will pass with the West hand. North might still double three hearts, but he would be making a very risky double. He has no idea whether his partner has any tricks or any hearts. He doubled four because he knew the players, and he was doubling a hand which was in game anyway. This time he struck gold. West was unlucky to find East with such a hopeless hand, but he shouldn't have played him for more than eight points at the most. In the back of West's mind was the time the same East had bid three hearts with

♠ 4   ♡ 9 8 7 4 2   ◇ A 6 2   ♣ A 5 4 2

Learn to bid game on this hand, unless you enjoy playing contracts like the one above.

With both sides vulnerable, the bidding proceeds:

SOUTH	WEST	NORTH	EAST
3 ♡	double	pass	?

You are East, and hold:

(1) ♠ K 10 4 2   ♡ 5 4 2   ♢ 4   ♣ A 10 6 3 2
(2) ♠ J 4   ♡ A 4 3   ♢ K Q 9 8 3   ♣ 10 5 3
(3) ♠ J 4 2   ♡ 10 5 3   ♢ 10 7 6 4 2   ♣ 6 3
(4) ♠ A 3   ♡ Q J 4   ♢ 7 6 3 2   ♣ 7 6 3 2

Bid four spades on hand (1). When partner makes a double of three hearts, he promises support for spades. Your hand
and your suit are both quite good enough to play a spade game.
A cue-bid is out because partner may bid five diamonds, and
a four-club bid is hopeless. You would bid four clubs with a
worthless hand containing at least four clubs and less than four
spades. You shouldn't jump to five clubs, because partner promises good spades but might not have very good clubs. He would
have doubled three hearts with

♠ A J 5 3   ♡ 3   ♢ A K 8 7 2   ♣ K 5 4

but not with the spades and clubs reversed.

Three notrump is best on hand (2). You probably have
nine fast tricks, but even if you don't, you should be able to duck
two hearts and keep South out of the lead thereafter. Four diamonds doesn't show a thing, and five diamonds doesn't figure
to be as good a contract as three notrump. You should decide
against passing the double. They may make it, and if they don't,
your game in notrump should score more anyway.

Hand (3) is what preempts are all about. You're damned
if you do and damned if you don't. Bid four diamonds with a

conservative partner, and pass with an aggressive one. They'll probably make it, but by bidding you will probably go for a big dive.

Pass hand (4). They will almost surely go down, and you probably do not have a game. You may be missing a three-notrump game, but if you are, there's a good chance that they will go down at least five hundred.

Try not to pass with a weak hand, especially if you can bid a suit at the three level. Your partner should realize that you are weak and should not raise without a very fine hand.

When you are responding with a hand which is just on the borderline between a minimum bid and a jump, try to take the following ideas into account before making your decision:

(1)   Your partner's double will be solid if he is vulnerable.

(2)   When vulnerable against not vulnerable opponents, his double must be very good.

(3)   If neither you nor your right-hand opponent has passed originally, partner must have full values.

(4)   If you have passed originally and your right-hand opponent hasn't, partner should have extra values.

(5)   If you and your right-hand opponent have both passed originally, you must have a good hand to jump, since partner is playing you for some cards and may not have full values.

Responding to Four- and Five-Level Doubles

Unless you are responding to a *balancing* double of four of a minor, you should think first of passing four- and five-level doubles. Take the double out only when holding a distributional hand with a good suit. The hand will break badly, and your partner may not have good support for all the suits. When the opponents preempt, they are assuming that they will go down. When partner doubles, he says that he seconds the motion. So let them go down unless you have a good reason to bid. They have contracted to take at least ten tricks, and so will you if you bid.

Only in the following auctions should you rush to take out a double at the four level:

SOUTH	WEST	NORTH	EAST
4 ♣ or 4 ♦	pass	pass	double
pass	?		

Your partner should be doubling only with support for both majors and a good hand. He expects you to bid a major. If he was dealt a hand with good values in the opener's suit, he should pass and take his profit. He is not over the bidder. You should pass only with a trump trick and no major to bid.

RESPONDING TO DELAYED TAKEOUT DOUBLES AND DOUBLES AFTER BOTH OPPONENTS HAVE BID

The same principles apply to responses to these doubles as to the direct takeout double. You will have more information about your partner's holding, because on most occasions he will be asking you to bid only one of two suits. You will often have to bid a three-card suit, since you are being forced to choose between only two unbid suits. So when you do hold four or five cards in one of the suits, you should be prepared to jump with fairly light hands.

SOUTH	WEST	NORTH	EAST
1 ♡	pass	2 ♣	pass
2 ♡	double	pass	?

You, East, not vulnerable hold:

♠ 4   ♡ 4   ♦ A 7 6 4 3 2   ♣ 7 6 4 3 2

Bid five diamonds. Partner holds spades and diamonds and is short of clubs. You should have a good play for five diamonds, and the opponents can probably make four hearts.

You hold:

♠ Q 10 9 7 2   ♡ 3   ♦ J 7 6 4 2   ♣ 4 2

Bid four spades. The opponents have a sure game, and you have a cheap sacrifice. Bidding four spades immediately makes life difficult for them.

RESPONDING TO THE BALANCING DOUBLE

In most situations where your partner makes a balancing double—a double in the pass out position—he is counting on you to hold a few cards. You would jump or cue-bid only with good values.

SOUTH	WEST	NORTH	EAST
1 ♡	pass	2 ♡	pass
pass	double	pass	?

You would need a good suit and the equivalent of an opening bid to take violent action in this situation. Your partner couldn't bid over one heart. He is obviously bidding most of your cards when he balances. He knows that the opponents have found a fit and decided to stop at the two level. Rather than let them steal the hand, he is trying to find a fit at a low level or push them a little higher. Take it easy.

THE RESPONDER'S ACTION
AFTER A REDOUBLE

After an opening bid, a double and a redouble, the responder need not bid. His partner, the doubler, will rescue himself. This is the accepted practice in this most common auction. In other sequences involving doubles and redoubles, however, a pass by the responder will indicate that he wishes to play the hand there.

SOUTH	WEST	NORTH	EAST
1 ◇	pass	pass	double
redouble	pass	pass	?

East should pass! West was planning to pass the double, and you should not be run out just because South redoubled. West is over the bidder and could very easily have good diamonds. When he passes over the redouble, he says he does have them.

Had North raised to two or three diamonds on the first round, and had the rest of the bidding remained the same, East would still have passed. West says he wishes to defeat them. East should remove only with a highly distributional double.

A word of caution should be included here. Just as with the cue-bids, these sequences should be worked out with your favorite partners. With unfamiliar partners, don't blindly close your eyes and pass—unless you want the rubber to end in a hurry.

FURTHER TIPS FOR THE RESPONDER

There are several general principles which the responder to a takeout double should recognize. Keeping them in mind will go a long way toward producing a confident partnership.

(1)   When partner doubles, he says he has good defense as well as good offense. Don't get pushed around until you get to a contract you can't make. Opposite a takeout double, you will often end up in a position where you can double the opponents for penalties if they decide to compete at too high a level. Be ready with your hatchet.

(2)   If the opponents begin to bid a suit other than the one opened, you do not need good trumps to double. Partner has promised support for that suit when he doubled. If he has a bad holding in the suit, he should not stay for your double. Holding

♠ K Q 9 8 2   ♡ 5   ◊ A 6 1 2   ♣ J 7 3

you would double if the bidding came to you 1 ♠–double–2 ♣ The opponents are in trouble.

(3)   Try to develop a feeling for which side should play the hand. With scattered values, it is quite probable that neither side can make anything after a takeout double by partner. Give

the opponents a gentle nudge and then let them play. With a weak hand and a good suit, on the other hand, you should try to play the hand yourself. Partner has promised a good hand, and you have little defense. Both sides can probably make something, so you should attempt to play the hand even if you are a trick too high.

(4) Bid aggressively. As we mentioned previously, it is very expensive to have a partner who thinks he has to bid your cards. Get the reputation for aggressive action after a double, and you'll be way ahead of the game.

REBIDS BY THE DOUBLER AFTER
A MINIMUM RESPONSE

When you have doubled, you have shown an opening bid and have *forced* partner to bid. Unless your partner has jumped or has bid freely, any further bid by you shows a very good hand. You are getting your side to a higher level opposite a potential bust. This applies even if your rebid is at the same level, since partner may have to correct to a higher level. Therefore, if you double one heart and then bid two spades over your partner's two-diamond response, you are showing a hand which is at least as good as

♠ A J 10 8 4   ♡ K 3   ◊ A 8 2   ♣ K J 9

With less, you would pass to two diamonds! Partner has shown less than nine points.

We have made this point first because rebidding with minimum doubles is the most common error of the inexperienced player. There is a tendency to become excited when partner bids a suit in which you hold four with two honors. Remember, you have asked him to name a suit, and unless he makes some bid other than a minimum response, you should be happy that he has hit your best suit but not ecstatic enough to raise unless your hand is above the minimum range.

Your basic rebid is *pass*.

If you have doubled with a minimum, you should generally allow your partner to carry the ball thereafter. He may make a

minimum rebid and then later bid another suit. His hand has
not grown; he is merely telling you that he has heard your double and that he wishes to compete to whatever level *he* thinks
is safe. It is up to you to give him a preference in his suits, but
you should not get excited and jump, because he *expects* you
to hold four-card support for at least one of his suits.

Even if partner has made a jump response, there are many
hands with which you should pass. Your partner's jump is not
forcing and shows from nine to eleven or twelve points. If you
had doubled with a minimum, you would go on with good support for partner's major suit, but you would pass with only
moderate support and no distributional values.

If you are satisfied that you have learned to pass, you may
proceed. The next section is devoted to those who hold big hands
against opening bids.

Rebids Other Than the Pass

Raise in partner's suit:
Raising partner's suit after a non-jump response shows about
sixteen or seventeen points with four-card support. If your raise
must be made to the three level, you should have seventeen or
eighteen. These requirements apply even when your raise is competitive (1 ♡–double–pass–1 ♠–2 ◇–2 ♠).

If partner has jumped, you would raise with a minimum
only if you had four-card support. With a better hand and only
moderate trump support (Q 6 2), you would bid a new suit or
notrump.

Jump raise in partner's suit:
If partner has made a non-jump response, a jump raise would
request him to go to game with any four-card holding and a
trick in his hand. A typical raise from one to three spades after
a double of one diamond would be

♠ A Q 5 3   ♡ K Q 3   ◇ 3   ♣ A J 7 6 2

If partner has made a jump response, you would make a jump
raise with the same type of hand with which you would raise if
partner had made a non-jump response—for instance,

♠ A J 5 2   ♡ K J 6 2   ◇ 6 2   ♣ A Q 6

over a double of one diamond and a two-heart or two-spade response.

Bid of a new suit:

Bidding a new suit after a minimum response always shows a good hand. This bid does not deny support for partner's suit; it merely describes a hand which does not have four-card support for partner's suit but which is good enough to raise the level of the bidding while trying to get to the best contract. Don't bid a new suit just because partner bid the suit in which you had the least support. The higher the level at which you are forced to bid your suit, the better your hand must be. When bidding a five-card spade suit at the one level after a takeout double and a response by partner, your hand need not be as good as when your bid would have to be made at the two or three level. You cannot, however, bid a new suit with a minimum double.

SOUTH	WEST	NORTH	EAST
1 ◇	double	pass	1 ♠
pass	2 ♡		

In this sequence, your hand (West) should be something like

♠ Q 8 7   ♡ A Q J 7 4   ◇ A 4   ♣ K 10 4

East should then go back to spades with five spades and only one or two hearts. West should then *pass*. He has shown the strength of his hand with his first two bids. Partner merely prefers to play spades. (There are holdings—

♠ K 7 6   ♡ A K J 4 2   ◇ 5   ♣ A Q 6 3

for instance—with which the doubler might try once more with three spades, but these are exceptional.)

Jump in a new suit:

A takeout double followed by a jump in a new suit after a minimum response by partner indicates a hand that is just lacking the strength to produce a game. You would usually have a very good six-card suit, and partner should raise if he has any trick in his hand.

SOUTH	WEST	NORTH	EAST
1 ♡	double	pass	2 ♣
pass	3 ♠		

West's hand should look something like

♠ A J 10 9 6 2   ♡ 5   ◇ A K 4   ♣ A Q 8

As we shall see later, this hand is too strong for either a one-spade or a two-spade overcall and is just a little too good to double and then bid two spades. Partner should not be afraid to raise just because he has bad trump support. West's spade suit should not be worse than the one in this example. He merely needs some trick in partner's hand to produce a good play for game.

Cue-bid:

If you cue-bid the opener's suit after having originally made a takeout double, you are showing a good hand, and you are usually attempting to get a further clarification of your partner's hand. You cannot be bidding the opener's suit with the intention of playing there, since you have already denied length in that suit with your double. You may bid a suit which your left-hand opponent has mentioned, and in this case you would be showing a good hand and at least a good five-card holding in that suit. You would not be cue-bidding.

SOUTH	WEST	NORTH	EAST
1 ◇	double	pass	1 ♠
pass	2 ◇		

Either of the following hands would fit West's bidding:

(1) ♠ A J 5   ♡ A K J 4   ◊ 4   ♣ A J 7 6 2
(2) ♠ J 6 2   ♡ A K 3   ◊ 4   ♣ A K Q J 8 3

On hand (1) you would like to see if partner can make
any kind of a strong bid after your cue-bid. He has already made
a minimum response, so with a fair five-card spade suit, he
should jump to three spades. You would proceed to four. If he
bids two notrump, showing a diamond stopper, you would bid
three clubs. This is not a forcing bid, since you did not make a
cue-bid at your first opportunity. Partner would go on only if
he had a fit for your suit in addition to his diamond stopper.

On hand (2) you are hoping partner can bid two notrump.
You have eight tricks in notrump, and if partner has diamonds
stopped, you should be a big favorite to make a notrump game.
You would raise two notrump to three, or you would bid three
clubs over two of a major.

If, as the responder, you have made a minimum response
on your first turn, you should be prepared to jump or bid notrump even with very few values if your partner cue-bids after
doubling. He should have a very good hand, and anything you
have of value—a stopper in the suit opened or a decent five-card
suit—should be shown with either a notrump or a jump rebid.

Notrump rebids:
A notrump rebid after a minimum response by partner always
indicates a good hand—how good it is depends on the level at
which the bid is made.

> (a) 1 NT: This call indicates between fifteen and
> eighteen high-card points and denies four-card
> support for the suit partner bid. You must have
> a stopper in opener's suit and good support
> for an unbid major or majors. (Otherwise you
> would have overcalled 1 NT immediately.)

> (b) 2 NT: If partner's response was at the one
> level, you show about nineteen or twenty high-
> card points; if partner was forced to bid at the
> two level, your bid would indicate a good sev-
> enteen to twenty. If partner has bid a minor,
> notrump rebids by the doubler often show a
> fit, but if partner has bid a major, they usu-

ally show a bigger hand with lack of a good fit. Any of these bids shows at least one stopper in opener's suit.

(c) 3 NT: A very rare bid, it indicates either the equivalent of a two-notrump opening bid or a big hand with a big fit for partner's minor suit. (With a big fit in a major, you should either cue-bid or jump raise.)

Repeated double:

If you double on your second turn, you show a good hand. Your double is for penalties if your partner has bid; if he hasn't, it is again for takeout.

SOUTH	WEST	NORTH	EAST
1 ◇	double	pass	1 ♡
2 ◇	double		

This sequence would show a hand with which you were about to bid notrump over partner's heart bid—for instance,

♠ A Q 9 2   ♡ K 6   ◇ K 10 8   ♣ A Q 9 4

It is a suggestion to partner that two diamonds doubled is the best place to play.

SOUTH	WEST	NORTH	EAST
1 ◇	double	2 ♣	pass
2 ◇	double		

In this auction, West should hold something like

♠ K J 9 2   ♡ A J 7 2   ◇ 6   ♣ A K 7 3

West can never be holding a minimum, and just how good his hand should be depends upon the level and the vulnerability.

REBIDS BY THE DOUBLER AFTER
STRONGER RESPONSES

The doubler's job is made easy by many of the strong responses. In most cases the responder is describing and limiting his hand in one bid—a jump in a suit or a notrump bid, for instance—and the doubler is not obliged to bid with an absolute minimum and only a mild fit.

(1) ♠ Q J 4 2	♡ Q 9 7 6	◇ A K 4	♣ 4 2
(2) ♠ K J 4 2	♡ A 8 4	◇ A Q 4 2	♣ 4 2
(3) ♠ K Q 4 3	♡ Q 4 2	◇ A 10 9 5 3	♣ 5

SOUTH	WEST	NORTH	EAST
1 ♣	double	pass	2 ♡
pass	?		

Each of these hands should be passed. Partner has limited his hand with his jump. If you bid three diamonds with hand (3), you are not correcting the contract; you are showing a good hand with secondary support (such as Q 8 3) for hearts. Any bid by the doubler is forward-going.

If you, as the doubler, have a minimum with good support for partner's major or a good hand with mild support, you should raise one level. With better hands, you should go to game.

(1) ♠ Q J 4 2	♡ K 9 7 6	◇ A Q 4 2	♣ 2
(2) ♠ A J 4 2	♡ A 10 4	◇ A Q J 2	♣ 4 2
(3) ♠ A K 9 3 2	♡ Q 4 2	◇ A Q 9 2	♣ 4

SOUTH	WEST	NORTH	EAST
1 ♣	double	pass	2 ♡
pass	?		

Hands (1) and (2) are three-heart bids. With another ace you would go directly to game.

Bid two spades on hand (3). You are not running; you are showing a good hand with at least five spades and some heart support. With the same distribution but fewer high cards, you would pass.

If partner has cue-bid, you are forced to bid until he stops naming new suits. With a good hand you should either jump if you have a five-card suit or cue-bid yourself to show a good hand and support for all suits. Your partner's cue-bid may have been on a fairly poor hand with support for both majors, so in order to make sure he doesn't pass your first rebid, you must show additional strength if you have it. With

♠ A J 8 3   ♡ A J 7 2   ◊ 4   ♣ K Q J 3

you would double one diamond and bid three diamonds over a two-diamond response from partner.

FURTHER TIPS FOR THE DOUBLER

(1)   The most important thing to remember is that when you double you show support for the unbid suits. You also show at least the value of an opening bid. Unless you have more than you showed with the double, don't bid again.

(2)   Lead trumps when partner passes your takeout double or doubles a sequence such as 1 ♡–double–2 ♡–double. Partner must have good trumps, and your objects should be to draw the declarer's trumps; and to stop a cross-ruff.

(3)   In auctions such as 1 ♡–double–3 ♡, partner may bid three spades with fairly light holdings. He realizes that the opponents are attempting to shut him out of the bidding, and he may be forced to bid with shaded values, such as

♠ A 8 7 5 2   ♡ 7 6 2   ◊ K 7 2   ♣ 7 2

He knows that if he passes your side may not be able to get to spades. You should not raise unless you have a good double with good spades. In crowded auctions such as these, the partner of the doubler will often be bidding on shaded values. In an auction like 3 ♡–double–4 ♡–4 ♠, you have no idea what the

four-spade bidder has. He may be saving, or he may have a reasonably good hand. He would make the bid either with

♠ 9 8 7 6 5 4   ♡ 4   ◊ J 7 6 2   ♣ 4 2

or with

♠ A K 8 7   ♡ 7 6 4   ◊ A 8 7 4 2   ♣ 2

When you get involved in sequences such as these, you will begin to see the value of preempts. Don't head for slam unless you
have a terrific hand with good distribution. Even if partner has
some cards, the suits figure to split poorly. If you are not sure
what's going on, it is usually a good idea to stop at game.

These last two chapters should have indicated the versatility
of the takeout double. It is your number one weapon. It is also
a delicate instrument, so use it carefully.

Quiz II—After the Takeout Double

SOUTH	WEST	NORTH	EAST
1 ♣	double	pass	?

You are vulnerable. What should you, East, do with the following hands?

(1) ♠ J 10 6 3   ♡ A 9 6 3 2   ◇ A   ♣ 7 6 3

(2) ♠ 8   ♡ K 8 7 3 2   ◇ Q 10 6 3 2   ♣ K 4

(3) ♠ 8   ♡ 8 7 6 2   ◇ 5 3 2   ♣ Q 9 8 6 5

(4) ♠ A 9 6 5 3 2   ♡ 4   ◇ A 6 3 2   ♣ 6 3

(5) ♠ K J 3   ♡ Q 4 3   ◇ 6 2   ♣ 8 7 6 3 2

(6) ♠ 6 3   ♡ 6 3   ◇ A K J 6 3 2   ♣ K 10 4

SOUTH	WEST	NORTH	EAST
1 ♠	double	2 ♣	?

With neither side vulnerable, what is East's best action with the following holdings?

(7) ♠ A 4 3 2   ♡ Q J 10 2   ◇ 6 4   ♣ 8 3 2

(8) ♠ Q J 10 6   ♡ 4   ◇ A 8 4 3 2   ♣ K 5 3

(9) ♠ A 3   ♡ 4   ◇ K Q J 9 8 3 2   ♣ J 5 3

(10) ♠ J 4   ♡ 8 6 3   ◇ 8 6 3   ♣ Q J 9 4 2

You are vulnerable. You deal, and the auction proceeds:

SOUTH	WEST	NORTH	EAST
			pass
3 ◇	double	pass	?

What should you do with the following holdings?

(11) ♠ A J 7 3 2	♥ 4 2	♦ 5 2	♣ Q 4 3 2
(12) ♠ K 5 3 2	♥ Q 10 4 3	♦ 5 2	♣ Q 4 3
(13) ♠ Q 4 2	♥ J 4 2	♦ 7 6 3	♣ 10 4 3 2
(14) ♠ K Q 9 8 6 2	♥ 4	♦ A 5 3	♣ J 10 4
(15) ♠ 10 5 3 2	♥ 6	♦ A 5 3	♣ K Q 7 3 2

You are now West. After first making a takeout double, what action should you take if the auction proceeds:

SOUTH	WEST	NORTH	EAST
1 ♣	double	pass	1 ♠
pass	?		

(16) ♠ Q 4 3	♥ A K 8 6 2	♦ K J 2	♣ 3 2
(17) ♠ A 6 4 2	♥ A J 8 6	♦ K 8 2	♣ K 4
(18) ♠ A 6 4 2	♥ A J 8 6	♦ K J 2	♣ 6 2
(19) ♠ A 6 4	♥ K Q J 6 3	♦ A Q 4	♣ 6 2
(20) ♠ A K 9 6 3	♥ A 4	♦ K Q 7 6 2	♣ 6

Answers—Quiz II

(1)	2 ♣	You intend to be in game in a major. If partner replies with two of a major, you would raise to game. If he responds two diamonds, you would bid two hearts (forcing).
(2)	2 ♥	Your hand is almost too good to make this non-forcing jump. Partner will pass with a minimum or with mediocre heart support.
(3)	1 ♥	Your trump holding must be better than this in order to pass partner's double.
(4)	4 ♠	Your hand is limited, so you don't cue-bid first. This hand will have a good play for four spades opposite any minimum double.

(5) 1 ♡   If no four-card or longer suit is available, and if your hand lacks the requirements for a one-notrump response, bid your cheapest three-card suit.

(6) 3 NT   Why announce to the opponents where your strength lies? Three notrump should be your best contract, so bid it. Partner *should not* take this bid out to four of a major unless he knows he can make it opposite a singleton trump.

(7) 2 ♡   This bid is highly competitive, and the doubler should not assume you have a better hand than you actually have. In fact, the two-club bid was helpful, since you were going to have to make a minimum response of two hearts. Now, at least, your bid shows some amount of strength, and the doubler can raise with a bit more assurance if he holds a good hand.

(8) Double   They are in trouble. North was afraid that one spade doubled was going to be passed. They may be going down anywhere between three and nine hundred. Remember, partner has shown some club strength with his double.

(9) 3 NT   You have too much for a three-diamond bid. (You would bid that without the ace of spades.) They may be able to run the clubs. but the chances are that three notrump is a laydown.

(10) Pass   South almost surely has a huge spade suit. Don't double two clubs and then wonder what to do when partner doubles two spades or bids more.

Problems with (1) *through* (10) *can be solved by referring to "Responding to the Direct Takeout Double" and "Further Tips for the Responder."*

(11) 4 ♠   Since you are vulnerable, and since you are a passed hand while the person to your right isn't, partner must have a *very* good hand to double. Your hand should make four spades a cinch. Reverse the vulnerability, and have the person on your right pass originally, and you would bid just three spades, since partner may have a rather light double.

(12) 4 ◊   Your hand rates a game for the same reasons as (11).

(13) 3 ♡   If you are normally aggressive in these situations, partner will not go on with doubtful hands. Playing with a bad player, you should pass the double and hope you can beat them.

(14) 4 NT   Six spades should be on if partner has two aces.

(15) 3 NT   Four spades could be better, but the preempt has used up your bidding space. Three no-trump seems your best chance for game.

For discussion of (11) through (15), see "Responding to Doubles of Preempts."

(16) Pass   Two hearts would show a better hand than this.

(17) 2 ♠   You hold the perfect raise.

(18) Pass   You need hand (17) to raise.

(19) 2 ♡   A takeout double followed by a new suit shows a good hand.

(20) 4 ♠   Partner bid the suit furthest from clubs, so he figures to have four or more spades. What else do you need?

For discussion of (16) through (20), see "Rebids by the Doubler after a Minimum Response."

5

The Overcall

♠ ♡ ◇ ♣

At present, 98.37% of all bridge players fall into the category of "bad-card holders." Of these, .001% decide to give up the game, and the rest resign themselves to their role and, aside from an occasional loud moan, struggle along as best they can. Our job in the next two chapters will be to end the exodus and keep the moans down to a low roar. You will still be bad-card holders, but you will be able to bear your burden more easily. In short, you will be able to bid more often and with better results.

When you consider the overcall, you should think of one word—"offense." More correctly, when you consider simple overcalls other than notrump, your instinctive reaction should be "offense." (All levels of notrump overcalls will be treated in a later chapter, because they are a breed separate from the suit overcalls.) When considering the takeout double, you think in terms of good hands both offensively and defensively, but in considering the suit overcall, you should think in terms of playing value and not worry about defensive values. You may, on the odd hand, be forced to overcall with good defensive cards, but you should be aware that such a case is an exception. In most cases, you overcall with the following objectives:

(1) To show a good suit
(2) To indicate a lead
(3) To prepare for a save
(4) To crowd the opponents' bidding
(5) To indicate offensive value in the suit bid
(6) To deny defensive or offensive values in other suits

It would be nice to be able to set up some specific upper and lower limits for the overcall, but in this case point count, unfortunately, is not an accurate gauge; the appropriateness of an overcall depends upon various factors. These *limiting factors* are:

(1)   The vulnerability
(2)   The level at which you are forced to bid
(3)   The sanity of your partner

No aspect of bridge is so closely related to your judgment of what you have to gain versus what you have to lose as the question of whether or not to overcall. A simple overcall—bidding a new suit at the cheapest possible level—can be made with as few as six high-card points and as many as fifteen or sixteen. Point count is of virtually no importance, however; your main concern should be fulfilling the six previously mentioned objectives at the minimum risk. The risk is determined by the three limiting factors.

Minimum values for an overcall vary according to the situation. You might bid one spade over one club with as little as

♠ K Q J 8 7 2   ♡ 8 2   ◇ 8 7 3   ♣ 4 2

if you are not vulnerable, but when you are vulnerable and opponents are not, you wouldn't bid two clubs over one spade with less than

♠ A 3   ♡ 6 2   ◇ 8 7 2   ♣ A K J 9 8 2

Without the ace of spades, you would pass, because by bidding you would be risking too much with too little chance of gain. Any time you overcall when vulnerable against non-vulnerable opponents, you risk a penalty and lose the advantage of preparing for a save. (There are very few cases in which a sacrifice is profitable at that vulnerability.) With the understanding that the values for an overcall vary, we can proceed to an examination of what an overcall should look like in different situations.

In almost all cases, overcalls are made with either one-suited or two-suited hands. Of these, the vast majority are one-suited. A one-suited hand is one in which you have very little strength except for a good six-card suit or a very good five-card suit—for instance,

♠ 7 2   ♡ K J 9 8 7 2   ◊ A 5   ♣ 8 7 2

or

♠ A K J 10 4   ♡ 7 2   ◊ 7 2   ♣ 8 5 4 2

A two-suited hand will usually have at least two five-card suits, although you may, on occasion, overcall with a five-four two-suiter—for instance,

♠ A J 10 8 2   ♡ 7 2   ◊ K J 9 6 2   ♣ 4

or

♠ A K 10 8 2   ♡ 6   ◊ K Q 7 2   ♣ 8 7 2

over one club. With equal-length suits you would bid the higher-ranking first, while with unequal ones you would usually bid the longer first. In all cases, there is an upper limit to how good your hand should be. If your hand warrants a double followed by a bid of your suit, you should do just that, and if your hand warrants a jump overcall, you should, as we will see in Chapter Seven, use that route.

You are dealt either a one- or two-suited hand, and the person to your right opens. In time you will develop an instinct which will tell you immediately whether or not to overcall. That instinct will be either right or wrong depending on whether or not you develop it correctly. It is much easier to develop it correctly than to change, so if you can try to keep in mind the six objectives and the three limiting factors, we will try to start you out on the best path.

With neither side vulnerable, South, the dealer, opens with one heart. What should you, West, do with each of the following hands?

(1) ♠ 9 5	♡ 9 5	◇ K Q J 8 7 3	♣ K 4 2
(2) ♠ 9 5	♡ 9 5	◇ A Q 7 6 3	♣ A Q 4 2
(3) ♠ 9 5	♡ 9 5	◇ K Q J 8 7 3	♣ 8 4 2

Hand (1) qualifies perfectly for a two-diamond overcall. You lack a lot of high-card points, but a two-level overcall is justified on all counts.

Hand (2) is a clear-cut pass! Overcalling with this type of hand—scattered defensive values and a bad suit—is contrary to all the objectives of overcalling. You have more high-card points than on hand (1), but you have good defense and very bad playing potential. You don't want to save, and you are not even sure you want a diamond lead. If you get doubled, you will probably go down five or seven hundred points; furthermore, if your opponents play it, they probably can't make anything more than a part score. If your partner is in the habit of overcalling at the two level with this type of hand, get yourself a new partner.

Hand (3) should also be passed. If the opponents were vulnerable or if your suit were spades, I would recommend an overcall, but in this case, because of the level and the vulnerability you would need a better hand. This hand is still a better overcall than hand (2).

There are many hands which would rate a one-level overcall but not a two-level overcall. The higher the level at which you are forced to enter the auction, the better your minimum requirements must be. There are two good reasons for this: (1) you are bidding at a higher level and (2) you are competing in a suit cheaper than the one opened, a fact which cuts down the competitive value of your hand. (It is always nice to hold the spade suit, so that you can compete at the same level at which the opponents have bid.) Both of these reasons make it clear that you have less to gain and more to lose when overcalling at the two level, and so your minimum requirements must be raised. Hand (3) above is a good example of the difference between having to bid at the one and two levels.

ONE-LEVEL OVERCALLS

We have said that most overcalls are made on either one- or two-suited hands. For a one-level overcall the strength of the suit can be reduced to as little as Q J 8 7 4, especially when not vulnerable and when a second suit is held. With one-suited hands the suit should tend to be stronger, since if you run into a bad split, you will not have any place to run.

With neither side vulnerable, the player at your right deals and opens one club. Your guess.

(1) ♠ K J 9 8 2   ♡ 5 3   ♢ 6 2   ♣ A J 7 3
(2) ♠ K 7 5 3 2   ♡ J 3   ♢ Q J 4   ♣ K J 7
(3) ♠ K J 9 8 2   ♡ Q 5 3   ♢ A J 2   ♣ K 4
(4) ♠ K J 9 7 3   ♡ 4   ♢ K Q J 9 7   ♣ 3 2

Bid one spade on hand (1). You are not vulnerable, and your hand fulfills the objectives of overcalling admirably. *When judging whether or not your suit is adequate, you should place great value on the quality of your secondary cards* (in this case the nine and eight of spades). When considering a penalty double, the person sitting behind you will always consider the size of *his* secondary cards in your suit. If you have the ten, nine and eight, your opponent obviously does not have them, and you are unlikely to be doubled.

Pass hand (2). Again you have more high-card points than on hand (1), but your suit is bad, and you have defensive rather than offensive values. You should be delighted to let the opponents play this hand—unless they find a fit and stop at the two level, in which case you can balance with a double or a two-spade bid, depending on whether or not they have bid hearts. This hand should not be considered a one-suited hand, because you have no idea that you want a spade lead or that the hand should be played in spades. Hands with 5-3-3-2 distribution rarely make good overcalls even at the one level. The exception would be a hand with all its values in the five-card suit or a hand like

♠ A K J 7 2   ♡ 7 2   ♢ 5 4 3   ♣ A 7 2

where a double of one club is not attractive. (Remember, a takeout double followed by a new suit shows a good hand.)

Hand (3) is a double. If you overcall with this type of hand, you are begging your partner to start responding with bad five-card heart suits. As we shall see in the next chapter, partner should not try a new suit over an overcall unless it is a good six-card suit. When you overcall with hands such as this one, you will not only be missing fits in other suits, but you will also plant a seed of doubt in partner's mind concerning your hand pattern on all succeeding overcalls. Your partner is not Houdini, so double when you have a double, and overcall when you have an overcall. Most important, pass when you have neither.

Overcall one spade on hand (4). With a two-suited hand, bid the higher-ranking first and the other one next if the level is not too high. (With this hand, you would try to get in a diamond bid short of the four level.)

It is not always a disaster to go down three hundred or five hundred after making an overcall. Depending on how much the opponents could have made, it may even be a considerable victory. But going down a lot at times when the opponents can't make a game *is* a disaster. This situation, commonly referred to as a "phantom save," is very often the consequence of overcalling with hands such as number (2). You have the defensive potential to defeat a game contract but lack the offensive potential to avoid a large penalty. And this brings us to a very important point: *you do not have a bid every time you have twelve or thirteen points, and you need not pass every time you hold as little as six.* Nothing is as aggravating as a partner who overcalls, goes down eight hundred against no more than a part score and then, very smugly, tells you that he had to bid because he had thirteen points. He had thirteen points and no competitive bidding judgment. Points have almost nothing to do with the question of when and when not to overcall, so if you find yourself in the position of having to explain a disaster to partner, tell him anything except how many points you held.

What all this amounts to is that a one-level overcall can be made with as little as

♠ Q J 9 8 5   ♡ A 4   ◊ 7 6 5 4   ♣ 3 2

when not vulnerable against vulnerable opponents, with the minimum values being raised by about an ace or king for each

change in the vulnerability (i.e., you would need one more
for neither side vulnerable, two more for both vulnerable,
finally three more for vulnerable against not vulnerable).
additional small card in the suit is also an added value, so that
adding the king of spades to the above hand would have the
effect of adding two values (a king and a sixth card in the suit).
With

♠ K Q J 8 7 5   ♡ A 4   ◇ 7 6 5 4   ♣ 2

I would overcall with any vulnerability. The presence of a very
good suit, such as this spade suit, should sway you to overcall
even with minimum values.

TWO-LEVEL OVERCALLS

Don't overcall at the two level unless you have a good
six-card suit (such as Q J 9 8 6 2) or better, or unless you have
a good five-five hand. With favorable vulnerability (not vulnerable against vulnerable), you may, about twice a year, get a
hand which warrants a two-level overcall with a five-card suit
and no side suit, but you must recognize that this is the exceptional case. An example would be the following hand, with which
you would overcall over one of a major:

♠ 7 2   ♡ 7 2   ◇ A 7 6 2   ♣ A K J 10 7

Because you are bidding at a higher level and bidding a
suit lower than the one opened, you have less to gain and more
to lose than when overcalling at the one level. You should,
therefore, have sounder values, especially in the quality of your
suit. Your secondary cards assume primary importance. Most
overcalling disasters occur when a person shades the values in
his suit in deference to strength in some outside suit. Remember,
the added outside strength you may hold could be just enough
to defeat any game the opponents may bid, and the lack of a
good suit may be enough to induce a penalty double from your
left. Result: an eight-hundred-point penalty and some mumbled
comment about thirteen points.

Therefore,

♠ K 3   ♡ 8 2   ◇ A K Q 7 6 2   ♣ 7 6 2

is a two-diamond overcall over a major with both sides vulnerable, but

♠ K 3   ♡ 8 2   ◇ A Q 7 6 3 2   ♣ K 7 6

is not. You would make a non-vulnerable overcall with the second hand, but with

♠ K 3 2   ♡ 8 2   ◇ A Q 7 6 3   ♣ K 7 6

you should not bid, regardless of vulnerability.

Minimum values would be approximately

♠ 8 2   ♡ 8 2   ◇ A K J 9 8 2   ♣ 8 3 2

with favorable vulnerability, and

♠ 8 2   ♡ 8 2   ◇ A K J 9 8 2   ♣ A J 8

with unfavorable. The vulnerability dictates all your overcalling decisions, and partner will play you for certain values depending on the vulnerability and the level at which you bid. With favorable vulnerability, for example, the second hand would rate as a minimum jump overcall. We will cover this topic in Chapter Seven.

When your hand rates a jump overcall or a double followed by a new suit, you should use those actions. It is extremely important not to overcall twice in the same suit without hearing from partner, so if you have enough for a jump or a double, you should use them. (The reasons for not overcalling twice in the same suit will be covered in Chapter Seven, but it should be understood here that there is a limit to how much you should have when overcalling.)

OTHER OVERCALLING SITUATIONS

There are countless situations in which you may have

difficulty deciding whether or not to enter the auction. In
Chapter Three we have mentioned many of these problems
separately, but when considering overcalling, we can include
them in one package.

As the level at which you are forced to bid rises, you should
be more and more aware of the vulnerability, and the value of
your suit—both in length and strength—should be correspond-
ingly high. From the three level upward, you should regard a
five-card suit with the utmost contempt, and only on very rare
occasions would you overcall with one. If you do overcall with a
five-card suit at a high level, you should have a second suit, and
the bidding should have proceeded in such a manner that a
takeout double or "unusual notrump" overcall (Chapter Eight)
would not apply. (If you hold the two suits that the opponents
haven't bid, you would normally use one of the devices just
mentioned.)

There is a certain finality about overcalling at a high level.
If, for example, your right-hand opponent opens with a three
bid, an overcall on your part eliminates the chance of penalizing
them and also makes it difficult for your side to play in any
suit other than the one with which you overcall. Furthermore,
if your overcall happens to be four of a minor, you preclude
the chance of playing three notrump. A takeout double has far
greater versatility, so use it if your hand qualifies or if you think
it is on the borderline between doubling and overcalling. Overcalling three notrump after a three opening will be discussed in
the chapter on notrump overcalls, but we may mention here that
it often takes the place of an overcall of four of a minor.

In all high-level situations the vulnerability is of prime
importance. Consider the following auction:

SOUTH	WEST	NORTH	EAST
1 ♠	pass	2 ♠	3 ♡

If someone were to ask you what the three-heart bidder's
hand should look like, you should excuse yourself or talk about
the weather. Without knowing the vulnerability, this sequence
is impossible to discuss. With just the opponents vulnerable,

East should have something like

♠ 4   ♡ A Q J 9 8 3   ◊ 8 7 6 5   ♣ K 3

but with just his side vulnerable, he would have to have at least

♠ 4   ♡ A Q J 9 8 3   ◊ A Q J 8   ♣ 3 2

In the first situation you can afford to enter the auction to set up a possible save and to suggest a lead, but in the second situation you can come in only if you think there is a good chance that it is your hand for either three or four hearts. In the one case, you are probably too high as soon as you overcall, in the other you are actually attempting to get to game. If you held the second hand and you were not vulnerable, you would double and then bid hearts—up through the four level if necessary.

If you are considering overcalling when there is an opening bid to your left, a pass by partner and a two-over-one to your right, you should have a very good six-card suit, regardless of the vulnerability. The opponents have good hands, and they may not have a fit. It is very likely that they will stop and double you if they are short in each other's suits. If you wander into this type of auction without a good suit, you will wind up with large penalties whenever the opponents can't make anything, and you will accomplish little when they can. Only if you have the spade suit should you bid on borderline hands.

SOUTH	WEST	NORTH	EAST
1 ♡	pass	2 ◊	2 ♠

Unless you are the only ones vulnerable, you would bid two spades with as little as

♠ A Q 9 7 6 2   ♡ A 4   ◊ 2   ♣ 10 8 7 2

A good save is not unlikely, since you can save at the same level as the opponents' probable game. The possible gain justifies the risk involved in a two-spade bid.

THE BALANCING OVERCALL

You are dealt

♠ K 8 7 4 2   ♡ K 6 2   ◊ A 5 2   ♣ J 4

and the person to your right opens one heart. Regardless of the vulnerability, your best action is to pass. This does not mean that you must stay out of the auction forever, it merely means that you have no reasonable action to take over one heart. With hands such as these—scattered values and a bad suit—it is best to pass at your first turn if you lack the values for a takeout double. If the player at your left raises to two hearts and the next two players pass, you should then bid two spades. The opponents have found a fit and stopped at a low level. Your partner surely has some cards and probably has a fit for spades. This balancing overcall by you describes a fair defensive hand with a mediocre suit. (With a good suit, you would have over-called at your first turn.) Lacking the distribution for a balancing double, you balance with a suit in this type of auction and in auctions when a one opening is passed around to you.

SOUTH	WEST	NORTH	EAST
1 ◊	pass	pass	?

(1) ♠ A Q 9 6 3   ♡ K 3   ◊ Q 7 4 2   ♣ 6 2
(2) ♠ A Q 9 6 3   ♡ K 3 2   ◊ 7 4   ♣ Q 6 2
(3) ♠ 4 3   ♡ A J 8 3 2 ◊ Q J 4 2   ♣ Q 6

Bid one spade on hand (1). If you double, partner will probably bid one heart, and your hand is not good enough to correct to one spade. Double has little to gain, because considering your diamond holding, your partner will almost surely not want to pass one diamond doubled for penalties. With any less than you hold here, you should pass one diamond. Partner had a chance to bid over one diamond and didn't. He probably doesn't have too good a hand. He may have scattered values and not enough to double.

Double with hand (2). Partner may be sitting with a good hand and good diamonds, in which case he will pass your double. If he bids one heart, you will pass.

Pass hand (3). What happened to spades? Partner couldn't overcall one spade, so the opponents very likely have a good spot in that suit—perhaps even a game. In any case, one diamond probably is not their best contract, and if you bid one heart, South figures to either bid spades or double for takeout. Don't balance in futile situations, and this one looks futile.

Be very careful about balancing after the opponents have stopped and have not found a fit. It is suicide to enter the auction with a bad suit after the following bids:

SOUTH	WEST	NORTH	EAST
1 ♠	pass	1 NT	pass
pass	?		

North's suit, or suits, is an unknown quantity. If you balance and run into one of North's suits, you will get doubled and go down plenty against nothing. You must listen carefully to the auction in order to gauge correctly the risks involved in sticking your nose in. As simple an auction as the one above can be very dangerous, while a more involved one like the following may cry out for a balancing bid in spades.

SOUTH	WEST	NORTH	EAST
1 ♡	pass	1 NT	pass
2 ♣	pass	pass	?

South has shown at least five hearts and four clubs. North has indicated less than ten high-card points and has denied holding four good spades. (Knowing your opponents is helpful in these situations. Some partnerships will never pass up any four-card spade suit, while most others will not pass up a good four-card spade suit.) Unless you run into the unlucky lie of three spades to your left and four to your right—a terrific long shot—you should be safe in making either a balancing double or a two-spade bid.

SOME CONCLUSIONS

Overcalling sequences can be lots of fun. You may, by overcalling, prepare for the defeat of the opponents' final contract by inducing the best lead from partner. You may be able to push the opponents too high by competing in your suit. You may wind up with a small loss instead of a big one by finding a good save. You may even get doubled in a save and end up making it because of tremendous distribution. You may keep them out of an otherwise biddable game.

Overcalling sequences can also be misery. You may, by overcalling on the wrong type of hand, get doubled immediately and go down a large amount when the opponents have no game. You may get the lead in your "suit" when you actually could have defeated the hand with the lead your partner would have made had you not overcalled. You may wind up taking a phantom save, because your partner believes you have a good suit and limited defense when you overcall. You may miss a good save the next time, because your partner remembers the last disaster.

When you overcall, have offensive (trick-taking) values with a good suit or suits.

Quiz III—Overcalls

With neither side vulnerable, your right-hand opponent deals and opens one heart. What is the first call you would make to describe the following hands?

(1) ♠ A Q 8 7 3   ♡ 6 3   ◇ A K 4   ♣ 7 6 2
(2) ♠ Q 6 3 2   ♡ K 4 3 2   ◇ K Q   ♣ A 10 4
(3) ♠ 6 3   ♡ Q J 4   ◇ A K 8 7 3   ♣ Q 6 2
(4) ♠ 6 3   ♡ 4   ◇ J 10 6 3   ♣ A K J 8 7 4
(5) ♠ Q J 9 8 2   ♡ 3   ◇ A Q 9 8 4   ♣ 4 2
(6) ♠ Q 6 3 2   ♡ 6 3 2   ◇ A Q 7 6 2   ♣ A

You are vulnerable, and your right-hand opponent deals and opens with one heart. What should you do with the following hands, and why?

(7) ♠ Q 6 3   ♡ 6 2   ◇ A K 8 6 4 3   ♣ K 4
(8) ♠ K Q 10 9 6 3   ♡ J 4   ◇ A 6 2   ♣ 6 2
(9) ♠ J 10 6 2   ♡ A   ◇ K Q J 9 8 6   ♣ 4 3
(10) ♠ Q 6 3   ♡ 6 2   ◇ A J 3   ♣ A Q 7 6 2

What is wrong with overcalling on the following hands after a one-diamond opening bid to your right? Neither side is vulnerable.

(11) ♠ A K 6 3 2   ♡ Q 4 2   ◇ 6 3   ♣ A 7 3
(12) ♠ J 8 2   ♡ Q 4 2   ◇ 6   ♣ K Q 9 7 6 3
(13) ♠ K J 3 2   ♡ Q 9 6 3 2   ◇ A J 4   ♣ 3
(14) ♠ Q J 4   ♡ K J 4   ◇ 6 2   ♣ A K Q 7 6
(15) ♠ Q J 10 8 7 6   ♡ A   ◇ 5 4 3 2   ♣ 6 2

Answers—Quiz III

All the questions in this quiz can be solved correctly if the six objectives of overcalling are understood and correlated with the three limiting factors.

(1)   Double   This call shows spades and support for the other suits. It also describes a hand with at least an opening bid and some good defensive values.

(2)   Pass   You have a good hand with very good defense, but you have too many hearts to make a double attractive, and you lack the requirements for a one-notrump overcall (see Chapter Eight). If hearts are raised, and two hearts is passed around to you, you might balance with two spades.

(3)   Pass   People who can't stay out of the bidding on these hands go broke eventually.

(4)   2 ♣   This hand fulfills all our objectives of overcalling.

(5)   1 ♠   With two suits of equal length which do not qualify for the "unusual notrump" (Chapter Eight), bid the higher-ranking first.

(6)   Pass   You may get a chance to make a delayed double if someone bids clubs.

(7)   Pass   A penalty double will prove very annoying —especially to your partner. You have a good defense and a doubtful offense, so the risk is too great to justify whatever small gain a two-diamond overcall may bring.

(8)   1 ♠   At least you can compete at the same level.

(9)   2 ◇   This is close, but you can expect to take at least six tricks, and you may need a diamond lead to defeat a notrump game.

(10) Pass   You don't have enough to double, and two clubs is *impossible*. (Don't make minimum doubles without good support for the other major.)

(11)   Everything is wrong; you should double.

(12)   The level is wrong; the limiting factors dictate a pass.

(13)   You have no suit, and your hand is not right for a double. You should pass and hope to get in a delayed double.

(14)   As in (11), everything is wrong with an overcall. Double stands out.

(15)   Nothing is wrong; you should overcall one spade.

6

After the Overcall

♠ ♡ ◇ ♣

When your partner overcalls, he is interested in playing the hand in the suit or suits he mentions; he is not interested in playing in some other suit or in doubling the opponents. Two things are to be concluded from this:

(1)   You should think first about finding a raise for your partner's suit and suppress the urge to bid a broken suit of your own.

(2)   You should be wary of doubling the opponents on the strength of partner's overcall. Or, as Lew Mathe told me when we started playing just prior to the 1962 World's Championship, "Kid, when I overcall, I want you to check your pistol at the door."

When your partner makes a takeout double, he is telling you that he would like to hear about your suits; when he overcalls, he says that he would not. *Your first, second and third thoughts should be to raise your partner's suit.* Of course it is not forbidden to play in some other suit or in notrump, but in order to try these other contracts, you must have either a very good suit or a very good hand or both.

Responding to an overcall is rather a standardized affair, so let's see what your actions should be after overcalls at various levels. Your responses change slightly according to the level at which your partner overcalled, since the level of his bid dictates the strength he must hold. The vulnerability must also be considered when trying to determine the correct response: partner must have a better hand to overcall vulnerable, so you can bid on a little less.

AFTER A ONE-LEVEL OVERCALL

Although your responses remain virtually the same regardless of the action of your right-hand opponent, we will first discuss your best actions in auctions that begin with an opening bid to your left, an overcall at the one level by partner and a pass to your right. As a guide, we will use the following auction:

SOUTH	WEST	NORTH	EAST
1 ◇	1 ♡	pass	?

There are four general groups into which your response can fall: the raise, the bid of a new suit, the bid of some number of notrump and the cue-bid. First things first.

Raising Partner's Suit

Since the strength of partner's overcall may vary considerably, it is up to the responder to clarify his own strength as quickly as possible, and the best way is to raise the suit which partner overcalled. In the above sequence, and in most sequences where you are going to raise your partner's suit, the vulnerability plays a very minor role, and your raise to the two, three or four level should adhere to the rules that follow. (Partner has taken the vulnerability into account when he overcalled, so when you raise with the same values, it has the effect of making your non-vulnerable raises a bit more preemptive—exactly the effect desired.)

Raising to the two level:

If, in the last auction, East were to bid two hearts, he would be describing a hand with at least three hearts and from six to eleven points. However, if he has ten or eleven points, his heart holding must be *no longer* than three—with four or more trumps and ten to twelve points in support of hearts, a three-heart bid would be correct. Do not hesitate to raise with six points and only three trumps. Even if the opponents wind up playing the hand, you may have made the bidding a bit more difficult for them, and you have told your partner that there are at least three hearts in your hand (a piece of information which may help him considerably on defense). You should not expect to be in a makeable contract every time you raise, but one of the main objects in overcalling is to set up saves. Another is to make life difficult for the opponents when it is their hand. You accomplish both of these aims when you get in a raise at your first opportunity. You also get it into your partner's mind that you will raise him even with minimum values, a very good idea indeed, since partners who get the opposite impression will very quickly get into the expensive habit of overcalling a second time in the same suit.

You may hold about nine points with three trumps and a five- or six-card suit on the side. We will discuss the bidding of a new suit shortly, but as a general rule, it is better to raise partner's suit if your hand is worth only one bid. With

♠ A J 8 7 2   ♡ Q 8 2   ◇ 7 6 2   ♣ 6 2

a raise to two hearts stands out. Partner is almost surely more interested in hearing about heart support than he is in hearing about some broken down five-card spade suit.

Raising to the three level:

A jump raise to the three level shows four- or five-card support and from ten to twelve points in support of the suit bid. (In this case a singleton rates as three points, and a void as four or five.) The popular term for this type of jump raise is *limit raise*. It is a two-way device, which serves as a preemptive action when partner has made a minimum overcall but constitutes a try for game when partner has overcalled with a good hand. If, in the example auction, East bids three hearts with

♠ 8 2   ♡ A J 7 2   ◇ K Q 10 8   ♣ 6 5 2

West will pass if his overcall is something like

♠ 7 4 3   ♡ K Q 10 9 8 3   ◇ 4 2   ♣ K 3

but will carry on to game with

♠ A 4 3   ♡ K 10 9 8 6 3   ◇ 2   ♣ K 7 4

Even if the jump raise results in a minus score, the result is
almost always a good one, since the opponents usually can make
something—often a game. In the first example, for instance, four
spades would be hard to beat. It is difficult to keep the opening
side from finding their spade suits in this type of auction, but if
you, as the overcalling side, happen to be dealt the spades, you
can very often keep the opponents out of hearts.

Here is a real life example of how to use the spade suit
and the vulnerability to frustrate the big-card holders (all your
opponents).

NORTH
♠ A 4 2
♡ A J 10 9 8 6
♢ J 9 8
♣ K

WEST
♠ Q 10 5 3
♡ 7 3
♢ A 4
♣ Q 10 9 8 2

EAST
♠ K J 9 8 6
♡ 4 2
♢ K 7 6 3
♣ 5 4

SOUTH
♠ 7
♡ K Q 5
♢ Q 10 5 2
♣ A J 7 6 3

North and South are vulnerable. The bidding goes:

SOUTH	WEST	NORTH	EAST
		1 ♡	1 ♠
2 ♣	3 ♠	4 ♡	4 ♠
5 ♡	pass	pass	pass

The opening lead of the diamond three defeats the contract
by one trick. Things won't always work out this well, but by

keeping the pressure on, you will achieve a good share of excellent results, such as this one.

It is because of the value of auctions such as the one above that the three-spade bidder must make his bid only on one type of hand—four- or five-card support of the suit bid. If he begins to jump raise with eleven or twelve points and only three-card support, the partnership will wind up saving on all the wrong hands. The overcaller will end up taking phantom saves because the responder will have too much defense and not enough offense for his jump.

Raising to game:

A jump raise to game in partner's overcalled suit should always be made on a hand with long (at least four) trumps and an otherwise highly distributional hand with a scarcity of high cards. It should resemble a response of four of a major over an opening bid of one of a major. With

♠ A J 8 7 2   ♡ 4   ◇ 4 2   ♣ Q 10 8 6 2

or

♠ K 5 4 2   ♡ 9 8 7 6 5 4   ◇ 4   ♣ A 2

you would bid four spades after a one-spade overcall.

With very big hands it is almost always better to cue-bid the opponents' suit and then go to game. In this way partner knows that you have a big hand, and he can make an intelligent decision about a possible slam or about what to do if the opponents decide to save. Again, bidding four directly has a preemptive effect, and if you have a big hand, you shouldn't care about preempting.

Raising competitively:

We have seen that a jump to the three level in partner's suit shows at least four-card support and from ten to twelve points. Situations develop, however, where you will be forced to raise at the three level without being able to jump.

SOUTH	WEST	NORTH	EAST
1 ♡	1 ♠	3 ♡	?

You, as East, may have been planning to jump to three spades. In this type of auction it is usually better to leap directly to four spades and reserve a three-spade bid for hands with three-card support and eight to eleven points. With pretty good defense it is safer to make this type of raise when vulnerable, since partner will usually not take a vulnerable save when South bids the expected four hearts. If you are not vulnerable and you are almost certain that you can defeat four hearts, you should not bid three spades in this type of auction. Partner will very likely take a phantom save on his next turn. Experience is invaluable in situations such as these, but you will be a year or two ahead of the game if you learn that you shouldn't bid three and then four spades in the above auction. You give the opponents one extra chance to gauge the position correctly. Bid four spades directly over three hearts if your hand calls for it.

We have discussed raises in partner's suit first, because it is far and away the most common action after an overcall. At least it should be. You have now learned at what level your initial raise should be. This information is worthless if the next rule is not followed. *Having raised partner's overcall, do not raise again in a competitive auction!*

SOUTH	WEST	NORTH	EAST
1 ♡	1 ♠	2 ♣	3 ♠
4 ♣	4 ♠	5 ♡	?

Unless you can double, you *must* pass. You have managed to put good pressure on the opponents and may have them one or two too high. Don't spoil all that good work by deciding to save. Partner heard your three-spade bid and decided to save at four spades. He may be going for five hundred, or he may be bidding it to make. Let him, the person with the undefined hand, make the last decision unless you are sure you can beat five hearts.

SOUTH	WEST	NORTH	EAST
1 ♠	2 ♣	2 ♠	4 ♣
4 ♠	pass	pass	?

Unless you can double, you *must* pass. Partner heard your clearly defined raise and decided to try to beat four spades. He could have taken the save but didn't. The fact that South bid four spades doesn't necessarily mean he can make it. He has been forced to make a decision at the four level which he would much rather have made at the three level in the form of a game try. You made it tough on him, and partner has voted, with his pass, to try to beat him. Don't make South happy by going for a three hundred or five hundred phantom.

There may be times when, after raising, the opponents will get out of the auction, and your partner will try to get to game. In these cases, you are free to raise again if you have a maximum for your bid.

SOUTH	WEST	NORTH	EAST
1 ♣	1 ♡	1 ♠	2 ♡
pass	3 ◇	pass	4 ♡

You may have had a very good two-heart bid; if so, when partner makes a further try at game, you would accept the invitation.

You may break the rule with one type of hand. If you have raised to the two level with a ten- or eleven-point hand and three-card support, and if the opponents go to the three level, you may raise again. You could not jump raise immediately, because you held only three-card support and a good defensive hand. You hold

♠ A J 3   ♡ 5 2   ◇ K J 10 4   ♣ J 9 8 5

and the bidding proceeds:

SOUTH	WEST	NORTH	EAST
1 ♣	1 ♠	2 ♡	2 ♠
3 ♡	pass	pass	?

This is the one case where you can raise again. You would

never, however, take a save after making a simple raise. You
have defense.

There are times when you should jump raise partner's suit
beyond game. With the opponents vulnerable, you pick up

♠ A 4 2   ♡ Q 9 8 7 6 5   ◊ 4 3 2   ♣ 2

and the bidding comes to you:

SOUTH	WEST	NORTH	EAST
1 ♠	2 ♡	3 ♣	?

Bid five hearts! The opponents have a game or a slam.
Take up as much bidding space as possible and let them guess.
If they go on to five spades or a slam, let them play. You bid
five hearts in order to make things tough—assume that you have
done your job and that they have had the chance to go wrong.
Maybe they have.

All of this discussion about raising the overcall is useless
if the overcall does not adhere to the principles set down in the
last chapter. If the overcaller has a hand with a bad suit and
scattered defensive values, this section on raises will create
havoc. Overcall correctly, and these raises will get the money.

Neither side is vulnerable, and the bidding proceeds:

SOUTH	WEST	NORTH	EAST
1 ♣	1 ♠	2 ♣	?

What should you, East, do with the following hands?

(1) ♠ J 10 2   ♡ J 4 3   ◊ A 9 7 3   ♣ 6 3 2
(2) ♠ Q 10 7 6 ♡ 5 2   ◊ A J 6 3   ♣ K 4 2
(3) ♠ 4 2   ♡ K J 6 4 3 ◊ K J 4   ♣ Q 10 5
(4) ♠ 9 7 6 3 2 ♡ 4   ◊ A 7 6 3 2 ♣ 5 3

Raise to two spades on hand (1). You couldn't have bid
with less than this, but you do not promise more. Failing to raise
will result in partner's thinking he must always try again with a

fairly good overcall. He will remember the times you didn't raise him with a hand such as this and will always be hoping to find you with something the next time you don't raise. Next time you will have

♠ 5   ♡ J 10 9 8 7 6   ◊ Q 6 2   ♣ J 7 2

and when partner tries spades a second time, he will go down seven hundred. It will be your fault. A raise may also have the effect of keeping them out of a heart game. Partner has implied short hearts and limited defense. A two-spade bid may find South with enough of a problem so that he won't risk bidding a bad four-card heart suit at the three level. So don't be a genius—just bid two spades and keep quiet thereafter. (You would also bid two spades if North had passed.)

Jump to three spades on hand (2). Your club king is badly placed, and that means that the opponents have a better chance of making something. Three spades describes your hand and makes things tough for South.

Pass hand (3). You will not always be right in this game. The object of a bidding philosophy is to get good results the majority of the time. Bidding two hearts or two spades could work on this hand, but more often it will not. You have scattered defensive values and lack a good fit for spades. Your suit is not good enough to bid at the two level. Don't mislead partner by bidding on this type of hand. The odd good result will not compensate for your undermining partnership confidence. This is the kind of hand where no one can make anything, so it is usually better to let them struggle. Save your competitive bidding for hands where both sides have fits.

Four spades stands out on hand (4). You probably can't make it, but the opponents can surely make something. Let them make up their minds at the five level without giving them the chance to find out about their heart fit. Who knows—you might even make four spades.

Bidding a New Suit

The best thing to remember about bidding a new suit after an overcall by partner is that since you are probably bidding a

suit in which partner has little interest, you should have about
the same values that you would have to overcall at the level at
which you are bidding. Therefore, in the auction such as 1 ♡–
1 ♠–pass–2 ◊ the two-diamond bidder should have a good six-
card diamond suit and an outside card. If your partner has made
a vulnerable overcall, your values may be just a good six-card
suit, since partner is showing good playing values for his overcall.

At the one level you may name a new suit with a good five-
card holding, the same as you would need to overcall at the one
level.

The bid of a new suit is in no way forcing and, if anything,
tends to deny a fit for partner's suit. You are showing a good
suit of your own and hoping partner has a better fit for your suit
than you have for his. If the level gets too high before you have
a chance to name your suit, it is better to stay out of the auction.
Partner is most probably not interested in your suit when he
overcalls.

If you have a choice between bidding a suit of your own
and raising partner's suit, it is better for partnership harmony, as
well as for points, to raise.

Even a jump in a new suit should be played as not forcing.
You would be describing a very good six-card suit and around an
opening bid, but your partner can pass if he has no fit and a
minimum overcall. (We will get to cue-bids, your only forcing
bids, in short order.) A jump bid in a new suit should also tend
to deny a fit for partner's suit.

With neither side vulnerable, you are East with the following hands:

(1) ♠ A J 9 5 3   ♡ 5 3 2   ◊ A 6 4   ♣ 6 3
(2) ♠ A Q J 9 7 2   ♡ 4 2   ◊ Q 4 3   ♣ 4 2
(3) ♠ A 2   ♡ 4 2   ◊ A K J 8 7 3   ♣ 5 3 2
(4) ♠ A 2   ♡ 4 2   ◊ A J 10 8 7 3   ♣ 5 3 2

SOUTH	WEST	NORTH	EAST
1 ♣	1 ♡	2 ♣	?

Don't bid two spades on hand (1). You can probably make two or three hearts, and you probably cannot make any spades. Bid two hearts where you are assured of at least an eight-card fit, rather than two spades where you may have only a six-card misfit. You should never bid suits such as this spade suit above the one level after an overcall by partner. Doing so will make it impossible for partner to know when he can compete in your suit. You should always have a six-card suit, and it should usually be a good one.

Hand (2) is a two-spade bid. If the opponents persist to three clubs, partner can compete in spades with a doubleton and a fairly good overcall. If, however, you have previously bid two spades with hand (1), you will find that partner will either sell out to three clubs or will rebid a five-card heart suit. Don't blame him. How is he supposed to know when you have your bid and when you don't? Even you don't know, and you're looking at the cards.

Jump to three diamonds on hand (3). Partner can pass with a minimum overcall and no fit. This is very important. With a bad diamond fit and a minimum overcall, partner *must pass* three diamonds. A three-heart bid would show a very good suit, and you would try four hearts. With a diamond fit and a stopper in clubs, the overcaller would bid three notrump. (We will see in the section on cue-bids that with a solid diamond suit and an outside ace, we would do something other than make a non-forcing three-diamond bid.)

Bid two diamonds on hand (4). You wouldn't mind competing a little with your hand, and by bidding two diamonds, you are telling partner that you have a fair hand with a good six-card suit and a limited fit for hearts.

Don't get trapped into bidding a broken suit at a high level when partner has overcalled. The bidding may come to you 1 ♡–2 ◊–4 ♡, with you holding something like

♠ K 8 7 6 4 2   ♡ 6 5   ◊ 6 5   ♣ A 6 2

In some cases a four-spade bid may be right, but most of the time it will be wrong—and expensively so. Partner should be making takeout doubles on most hands where four spades is the logical action, and he should be overcalling to show a diamond suit and a disinterest in other suits. We have separated the values for overcalls and takeout doubles to the extent that problems such as this one should cease to be problems. Pass!

Bidding Notrump

Any time you hold your share of the cards—ten or more points—and have limited values in partner's suit and some stoppers in the opponents', you may think of bidding some number of notrump. At what level you bid depends largely on the vulnerability, since partner is guaranteeing more strength when he overcalls vulnerable.

Keeping in mind that you must have at least one sure stopper in the opponents' suit and that you should have scattered values in the other unbid suits, here are the approximate ranges of notrump responses to one-level overcalls.

		Not vulnerable	Vulnerable
	1 NT	9-12	8-11
Competitive	2 NT	11-13	10-12
Jump to	2 NT	13-15	12-14
	3 NT	15-16	13-15

There is a difference between a competitive two-notrump bid and a jump, because the opponents will often open a suit and raise, and you will try two notrump on a hand which would not rate a jump to two notrump.

With neither side vulnerable, the bidding proceeds:

SOUTH	WEST	NORTH	EAST
1 ♣	1 ♠	2 ♣	?

You hold:

♠ J 3   ♡ Q J 9 2   ◇ J 10 7 6   ♣ A Q 9

You would have bid one notrump, but that bid is no longer available. You would bid a "competitive" two notrump.

However, point count is, as usual, only worthwhile as a guide on hands which are fairly square. With highly distributional hands or with hands where you have a long, solid suit, common sense will tell you that you require less point count to produce game. Therefore, with something like

♠ 5   ♡ 10 8 7 2   ◇ A   ♣ A K Q 9 8 5 2

you would bid three notrump after a one-diamond opening and a spade overcall by partner. (Three clubs is *not* forcing.)

While you may bid one notrump with less than ten points, it is often better not to. The hand probably doesn't belong to you, and a notrump bid will merely have the effect of making the hand easier for the opponents to play when they buy the contract. With ten or more points, however, you should bid, because partner may be able to compete effectively if he holds a fairly good overcall.

Any notrump response should alert the overcaller that you are interested in competing only long enough to get the opponents too high. You deny good trump support, so unless the overcaller has a second suit, he should be happy to defend if the opponents bid again. Since this is the case, the notrump bidder must make sure that his support for the overcalled suit is indeed limited. He should normally not have more than a doubleton honor, although there are hands where he may hold three small. We are dealing here with a judgment of which side should be allowed to play the hand. After a one-level overcall and a one-notrump response, you should be willing to push the opponents to the three level and then let them play. Nine tricks are usually not available to either side.

SOUTH	WEST	NORTH	EAST
1 ♣	1 ♠	pass	?

With neither side vulnerable, you, East, hold:

(1) ♠ Q 5 3	♡ K 10 4	◇ Q 10 4	♣ Q J 5 3
(2) ♠ —	♡ A J 4 2	◇ J 6 3 2	♣ K 9 8 6 2
(3) ♠ 4 2	♡ Q 4 3 2	◇ Q 6 3	♣ A Q 10 4
(4) ♠ 4 2	♡ A Q 4	◇ K J 5 3	♣ K J 8

One notrump is tempting on hand (1), but two spades is correct. Unless you want partner to begin rebidding five-card suits, don't poison his mind with thoughts about not getting a raise with three trumps to an honor.

Pass hand (2). Do not rescue partner because you hold no trump support. We are overcalling on good suits, and this hand will almost surely play better in spades than in notrump. A one-notrump bid will probably result in further spade competition, while a pass won't. A disciplined partner will not rebid his over-called suit unless you have made a bid.

A one-notrump response shows a fair hand, mediocre trump support, scattered values and at least one stopper in the opener's suit. Bid one notrump on hand (3).

Hand (4) is a standard two-notrump bid after a non-vulnerable overcall. But don't be too surprised if you can't even make two.

Bidding notrump after an overcall will be a good lesson on how few tricks are available in notrump on misfit hands. Don't shade your values.

Cue-Bidding

If your partner opened the bidding one spade and you held

♠ K 8 5   ♡ 7 2   ◇ A 7 2   ♣ A J 9 7 2

you would bid two clubs, and your partner would have to bid once more. If you held the same hand and your partner over-called one spade, you could not bid two clubs, since that call would show a good club suit and deny an interest in spades. You have too much to bid two spades, and the pattern is wrong for three or four. You should cue-bid the suit that was opened.

The cue-bid is used after an overcall in much the same way

as it is used after a takeout double, with the important difference that you would always have nearly an opening bid or more.

There are three general types of hands that are best handled with the use of the cue-bid. They are (1) the good hand with a fair or good trump fit, (2) the good hand which is a potential notrump game if partner has the opener's suit stopped, and (3) the big hand with a powerful major suit. Types (2) and (3) would always be more than opening-bid strength, while type one would approach it.

Cue-bidding with a trump fit:

If you hold a hand which fits none of the patterns for giving a raise in partner's suit, you may be forced to cue-bid and then raise. New suits after a cue-bid are forcing, but if you cue-bid and then raise partner's suit, you are only inviting him to go on. Therefore, if you again held

♠ K 8 5   ♡ 7 2   ◊ A 7 2   ♣ A J 9 7 2

and the bidding came to you 1 ◊ –1 ♠ –pass, you would bid two diamonds. You would then raise spades as cheaply as possible if you were not vulnerable, or you would jump raise if you were vulnerable. This hand should produce a game opposite a vulnerable overcall, but if you are not vulnerable, you should give partner one opportunity to stop. You would not make an immediate jump raise with this type of hand, because a jump raise is to be made with four-card support and from ten to twelve points.

Cue-bidding with a potential notrump hand:

You may be dealt a hand where you have too much just to bid or jump in a minor suit of your own. You may want to play three notrump if partner has a stopper in opener's suit.

Neither side vulnerable, the bidding proceeds:

SOUTH	WEST	NORTH	EAST
1 ♣	1 ♠	pass	?

You, East, hold:

(1) ♠ 4 2   ♡ 4 2   ◊ A K J 9 8 4   ♣ Q 3 2
(2) ♠ 4 2   ♡ A 2   ◊ A K J 9 8 4   ♣ 4 3 2
(3) ♠ 4 2   ♡ A 2   ◊ A K Q J 9 8   ♣ 4 3 2

On hand (1) you would bid two diamonds, and on hand (2) three diamonds. Neither of these calls is forcing, and unless partner has either a good fit or a very good overcall, there will be no game. But on hand (3), you can make three notrump if partner has a club stopper and either the heart king or the spade ace. (Even the ace-queen of spades will probably do.) Bid two clubs. If partner rebids two spades, you will bid three diamonds. If he persists to three spades, you will give up. Your three-diamond bid is forcing—a new suit after a cue-bid—so if partner can do nothing but make minimum spade rebids, you should let him out at three spades. It is obvious that the overcaller should be alert to bid notrump with a stopper in the opener's suit. He must be aware that his partner has a very good hand. He might even jump to four spades if his suit is very good.

Cue-bidding with a big hand and a big major suit:
Just as you may sometimes have a minor-suit hand that is too good to treat with a jump, so you may also have a major-suit hand. With

♠ A Q 10 9 7 2   ♡ 5 4   ◊ A J 4   ♣ 5 4

you would bid two spades if partner bid one heart over one club, but with

♠ A K J 9 8 3   ♡ 5 4   ◊ A Q 5   ♣ 5 4

you would bid two clubs and then bid spades. In sequences such as this one, the overcaller should be aware that he holds fine support if he has as much as a doubleton honor or three small in the responder's suit.

SOUTH	WEST	NORTH	EAST
1 ♣	1 ♡	pass	2 ♣
pass	2 ♡	pass	2 ♠
pass	?		

West, holding

♠ Q 4   ♡ K J 10 9 7 3   ◇ K 3   ♣ 6 3 2

should be delighted to raise spades. It is of the utmost importance
that the overcaller learn to picture the type of hand the responder
should have in this kind of bidding sequence. He must remember that the responder could have bid either one or two spades.
The fact that he didn't, but instead chose to cue-bid and then
bid spades, marks him with a very good hand with very good
spades. The queen and one spade should be just what he needs.

FURTHER THOUGHTS FOR THE RESPONDER

The number of different sequences that will face you when
you are responding to an overcall is almost unlimited. Your
partner may overcall in either a major or a minor and at either
the one or two level. Your right-hand opponent may pass or bid
to any level. We have discussed the most common situations that
occur after a one-level overcall, leaving a wide range of possibilities untouched. Since a complete study would tax the memory
of a good-sized computer, we will limit ours to a few general
hints and the understanding that competence in responding to
one-level overcalls will go a long way toward solving problems
in responding to other possible overcalls.

(1) You would respond to two-level overcalls in much
the same way as you do one-level overcalls, with the added
thought that partner has a six-card suit and a better minimum
holding than he would have had if he had made a one-level bid.
There are even times when you may have to raise partner in competition with as little as a doubleton. This is a distasteful practice, since partner will often take a push to too high a level when
the opponents compete further, but there are hands where you
have no choice.

SOUTH	WEST	NORTH	EAST
1 ♠	2 ♣	2 ♠	?

As East, you hold:

♠ 8 7 3   ♡ Q 7 6 3 2   ◇ A K 2   ♣ J 4

You would have to try three clubs here and hope that no one
has enough cards or distribution to bid again. If you pass, the
opponents will probably make two spades, and you are a favorite
to make three clubs. (The overcaller should not make an auto-
matic four-club bid if the opponents bid three spades. He must
have an excellent overcall to take another push when partner
raises in competition.) The biggest problem with a raise on a
doubleton is that partner may be induced to take a phantom
save if the opponents jump to game. Don't make doubleton raises
if there is a good chance that the person to your left will leap to
game. On the example hand, this possibility appears unlikely
because of your high-card strength.

(2)   Most partnerships have a great difficulty deciding
whether or not to rescue one another when doubled after an
overcall. In the style of overcalling which appears here, the
problem is negligible. Since overcalling with broken suits and a
lot of outside strength is barred, it is a good bet that the hand
should be played in the overcaller's suit, unless the responder
has a very strong suit of his own. As the responder, you should
not think of rescuing partner into a broken suit of your own.

SOUTH	WEST	NORTH	EAST
1 ♡	2 ◇	double	

With both sides vulnerable, you hold:

♠ Q 9 6 5 2   ♡ J 7 6 3 2   ◇ —   ♣ 10 4 2

You are ill, but you should pass. Partner may easily go down
eight hundred, but at least you can be assured that you have kept
the opponents out of a vulnerable game. Partner must have a
good six-card suit with limited cards in the other suits, especially
spades. In this case the result was down eleven hundred, and the

opponents would not have made a game. You, however, could have made two spades. Does this mean that the next time this situation arises you should rescue to two spades? I guess it does if you are playing with a partner who overcalls on

♠ K 4 3   ♡ Q 10 9   ◇ A Q J 5 2   ♣ A 5

and tells you afterwards, "But I had seventeen points, partner." This hand is exactly contrary to all the objects of overcalling. Either a double or a one-notrump overcall would be acceptable, but a two-diamond bid deserves to go down eleven hundred. If you overcall with this type of hand, expect to be rescued continually by skeptical partners.

(3) One of the objects of overcalling is to make life difficult for the opponents. Many opportunities will present themselves, especially when you are not vulnerable and the opponents are.

SOUTH	WEST	NORTH	EAST
1 ♠	2 ◇	2 ♡	?

You hold:

♠ 8 7 2   ♡ 4   ◇ A 7 6 4   ♣ K 7 6 5 3

You are not playing with the player who bid two diamonds on the previous disaster, so you can be sure that the opponents have a game somewhere. Bid five diamonds immediately and make them decide what to do without giving them the opportunity to get in some raises or jump raises. South may decide that the profit against five diamonds doubled is inadequate and bid five hearts. He may be wrong—who knows? You were going to bid five diamonds eventually, so why not bid it when it can cause the most trouble?

These are just three of the many different kinds of situations which you may encounter in an overcalling sequence.

These, and others like them, will be solved to your satisfaction if you overcall only on hands which fit the requirements. In almost all cases the responder is trapped into a horrible decision if the overcaller has a broken suit and scattered outside values. Don't overcall unless you have the requirements.

Quiz IV—After the Overcall

You are East in the following auction:

SOUTH	WEST	NORTH	EAST
1 ♣	1 ♡	1 ♠	?

With neither side vulnerable, what should you call with these hands?

(1) ♠ K 10 9 6   ♡ Q 5 3   ◊ J 4   ♣ A 9 8 3
(2) ♠ A 10 4   ♡ Q 6 3 2   ◊ J 9 8 6 3 2   ♣ —
(3) ♠ 7 6 2   ♡ K J 6 3   ◊ K Q 6 2   ♣ J 4
(4) ♠ 6 4   ♡ K 7 3   ◊ Q 10 8 6 3   ♣ Q 5 2
(5) ♠ Q 6 2   ♡ 6 3   ◊ A 9 6 3   ♣ K 5 3 2

The opponents are vulnerable, and you are not.

SOUTH	WEST	NORTH	EAST
1 ♣	1 ♠	pass	?

What bid best describes each of the following East hands?

(6) ♠ Q 8 3   ♡ A 10 7   ◊ A Q 9 6 2   ♣ 4 2
(7) ♠ 6 4   ♡ K Q 2   ◊ A Q 6 3   ♣ Q 10 6 2
(8) ♠ 6 4   ♡ A K 9 8 6 2   ◊ Q 6 2   ♣ 6 4
(9) ♠ 6 4   ♡ A K Q 9 8 6   ◊ Q 6 2   ♣ 6 4
(10) ♠ 6 4   ♡ A K Q 9 8 6   ◊ A 6 2   ♣ 6 4
(11) ♠ Q 6 4   ♡ A J 9 8 3   ◊ J 4 2   ♣ 6 4

Again the opponents are vulnerable, and you are not.

SOUTH	WEST	NORTH	EAST
1 ♡	2 ♣	2 ♠	?

As East, what is your best move?

(12) ♠ Q 10 9 6	♡ J 10 9 6	◇ A 4	♣ J 3 2
(13) ♠ 6 2	♡ 6 2	◇ A K 7 6 3	♣ J 6 3 2
(14) ♠ 6 2	♡ 6 2	◇ K 10 9 8 6	♣ A 5 3 2
(15) ♠ 6 3 2	♡ K Q 4	◇ 8 7 3 2	♣ Q 10 4

Answers—Quiz IV

(1) 2 ♡   A simple raise is perfect. You want to push them high enough so that you can beat them, and if partner bids three hearts, you should be able to make it. Don't bid one notrump and slow them up.

(2) 4 ♡   It is often hard to defend when they have the spades, but a four-heart bid could make life difficult for South. He may be looking at three-card spade support and be afraid to raise at the four level. If North later bids five clubs, you would pass and let partner decide what to do.

(3) 3 ♡   This is a standard three-heart bid.

(4) 2 ♡   Two hearts describes the hand, so bid two hearts.

(5) Pass   Do not bid one notrump every time you have nine points. Had North passed, you might have bid one notrump to keep them out of spades, but it is too late now. A one notrump bid will merely locate all the cards when the opponents buy the hand.

For discussion of hands (1) through (5), see "Raising Partner's Suit" and "Bidding Notrump."

(6)   2 ♣   Your hand does not qualify for any type of
                spade raise, so you cue-bid and then raise
                spades.
(7)   2 NT   Perfect.
(8)   2 ♡   This bid shows a good suit and a disinterest
                in the other suits.
(9)   3 ♡   Three hearts is not forcing, but it describes a
                hand with a very good suit and game possi-
                bilities.
(10) 2 ♣   You have too much for three hearts. If part-
                ner can bid two notrump, you will put him in
                three. Any other bid will allow you to show
                your heart suit.
(11) 2 ♠   Bid two hearts on hand (8), two spades on
                this one.

*Hands (6) through (11) fall under "After a One-Level
Overcall."*

(12) Pass   Don't raise in this type of auction with such
                a good defensive hand. Two spades is forc-
                ing, and it will be difficult for North and
                South to stop in time. Don't induce a phan-
                tom save by raising.
(13) 3 ♦   You should plan to take a cheap club save
                later, but you want a diamond lead if they
                go to the five level.
(14) 5 ♣   Make it as tough as possible as quickly as
                possible.
(15) 3 ♣   What's the problem?

*For discussion of hands (12) through (15), see "Further
Thoughts for the Responder."*

7

The Jump Overcall

♠ ♡ ◊ ♣

The jump overcall (1 ◊ –2 ♡) means different things to different people. To some, and for many years to all, this type of bid shows an enormous hand—the same hand which we would treat with a double followed by a jump. To others it shows a very weak hand with a six-card suit—a treatment known as the *weak jump overcall*. There are disadvantages to both these styles, and only the weak treatment offers any compensating advantages. The style of jump overcall which best fits our bidding methods puts the strength of the bid somewhere in between the strong jump overcall and the weak jump overcall.

The *intermediate jump overcall,* which is the name given to this bid in tournament play, shows a hand with about the strength of an opening bid, a good six-card suit, a disinterest in the other major or majors, and at least two defensive tricks. The minimum requirements vary slightly according to the vulnerability, but a two-heart bid over one diamond would look something like

♠ 7 2   ♡ A Q J 9 7 2   ◊ A Q 2   ♣ 7 2

Add the spade king, and you would double and then bid hearts. Add the ace and king of spades, and you would double and then jump in hearts. Take an ace away from the original hand, and you would simply overcall one heart.

There are several important advantages to playing your jump overcalls as intermediate. You fill a gap which exists between overcalling and doubling and then bidding a new suit.

You tell your partner in one bid that you have a good hand with a good suit—information which enables him to compete effectively as the auction progresses. Most important, you avoid the trap of having to overcall twice in the same suit in order to show the strength of your hand. The following hand is a very common example of the type of disaster which can be avoided with the use of the intermediate jump.

NORTH
♠ J 10 9 5
♡ 3
◇ 10 8 4
♣ J 9 8 6 3

WEST
♠ A K Q 8 7
♡ K 10 8
◇ 6 5 3
♣ 5 4

EAST
♠ 6 2
♡ 6 5 4
◇ K J 9 7
♣ A K Q 10

SOUTH
♠ 4 3
♡ A Q J 9 7 2
◇ A Q 2
♣ 7 2

With both sides vulnerable, the bidding proceeds:

SOUTH	WEST	NORTH	EAST
			1 ◇
1 ♡	1 ♠	pass	2 ♣
2 ♡	double	pass	pass
pass			

South goes down five hundred, and East and West could have made no more than a part score. South has gone against the principal idea of our bidding theory. He has allowed the

opponents an extra chance to decide what to do, giving them a
"free roll." It is true that by bidding two hearts immediately,
South would put himself in the same position to go for five
hundred, but would you, as West, double two hearts before
mentioning your spade suit? West would have to decide right
away that two hearts doubled is the best spot—an impossible
position to take at that point. When the bidding proceeds as in
the diagram, however, West has a very easy double of two hearts,
since he has already found out that no spade fit exists. It is easy
to say that South's second heart bid is awful, but he certainly has
a very good overcall, and even in the absence of a raise from
North, he figures that has hand could very well make two or three
hearts. By bidding two hearts immediately, South could have
described his hand and retired from the auction. The bidding
might then have died in two spades if East and West had worked
out that the two-spade bid is not forcing, but they might well
have gotten to three notrump if East had decided that he was
obligated to bid over two spades. North and South would then
have wound up with a profit instead of a five-hundred-point loss.
One can construct hands to fit any theory, but it has been my
observation that pairs, even very good pairs, that do not play
intermediate jump overcalls very often put themselves in situations such as this one. And an alert opposition will surely jump
on them when they are in trouble.

You may make a jump overcall to the two or three level,
but the bid applies only when you bid *one* more than you have
to. A three-diamond bid over one heart is an intermediate jump,
but a three-diamond bid over one club is preemptive. You would
bid two diamonds over one club to show a jump overcall.

Jump overcalls to the three level and vulnerable jump overcalls are about one king stronger than non-vulnerable jumps to
the two level. With

♠ 8 2   ♡ A 3   ◇ A K J 7 6 2   ♣ 6 5 2

you would bid only two diamonds over one heart. However, this
hand would also qualify for a two-diamond bid over one club.
Were you to add the spade king, you would bid three diamonds
over one of a major, but if you weren't vulnerable, you would

have a nasty problem bidding over one club. Your hand would
be a little too good for a jump overcall, but the two doubletons
in the majors would make a double followed by a diamond bid
unattractive. You would make a jump overcall and hope partner
can bid.

The jump overcall is quite specific, and partner can raise
with any doubleton. If partner makes a competitive raise, the
jump overcaller should not go on. He has described his hand
with his jump, and if partner wanted to be in game, he should
have bid game. Only after a non-competitive raise should the
overcaller consider going on. There is a vast difference, for example, between the following two auctions.

	SOUTH	WEST	NORTH	EAST
(1)	1 ♣	2 ♡	3 ♣	3 ♡
	pass	?		
(2)	1 ♣	2 ♡	pass	3 ♡
	pass	?		

In auction (1), East is unwilling to sell out to three clubs.
He may feel that his hand will allow West to make three hearts,
or he may prefer to go down one trick. He may even succeed in
getting the opponents to four clubs. West should pass even with
a maximum.

In auction (2), East is attempting to get to game. The hand
is already his, so his three-heart bid is a request for West to go
on if he has a maximum. With this same hand he would have
bid four hearts in auction (1), since three hearts would be
strictly competitive.

In all cases concerning jump overcalls, the responder must
pay strict attention to the vulnerability. Overcaller will have a
somewhat better hand when jumping vulnerable, so that responder can go on with less values.

Any new suit that responder bids after a jump overcall is
forcing. You do not bid a new suit just because you have a bad

fit for partner's suit. When a person makes a jump overcall, he has a suit that can play reasonably well even opposite a void. Bids of new suits are tries for game, and the partner of the over-caller should not introduce a new suit unless he has game aspirations. Don't bid two spades over a jump to two hearts with

♠ A J 10 9 8 2   ♡ 3 2   ◇ 7 6 5   ♣ 7 6

You might be able to make two spades, but you will not be able to play it there, since your bid is forcing. With an added ace you would bid two spades, and unless you got an immediate spade raise, you would go to game in hearts.

In most cases where you have made a jump overcall, it is best to let partner make the decisions when the competition gets to a high level. He is aware of your holding, but you are not aware of his. Consider the following auction:

SOUTH	WEST	NORTH	EAST
1 ♣	2 ♡	2 ♠	4 ♡
4 ♠	?		

Unless you can double, it is almost always right to pass. Partner may have put you in four hearts with a doubleton and good defensive cards, in which case he is waiting for a chance to double four spades. If he has a lot of hearts, he can bid five hearts. Bridge is a partnership game, so let the person who is in the best position to make an intelligent decision make it.

One of the really dangerous tactics in competitive bidding is the repeated overcalling of the same suit without a bid from partner. The hand with which you may justifiably do so comes up about twice a year, so if you have used up your quota, don't press your luck by going over it. The same thing applies after making a jump overcall. Don't butt in again unless partner has taken some action. If you are playing with a partner who will not support you when he should, get yourself a new partner—it is cheaper than trying to bid his cards for him. Don't bid three hearts in the following auction:

SOUTH	WEST	NORTH	EAST
1 ♣	2 ♡	3 ♣	pass
pass	?		

Partner had a chance to make a competitive raise. There is no reason why North can't have something like

♠ 8 2   ♡ Q 10 6 2   ◊ 7 6 5   ♣ A Q 7 2

You were in trouble in two hearts, but you didn't get doubled because North felt he should get in a club raise. Don't give him another chance to show his heart holding. One of the prime advantages of playing intermediate jump overcalls is that you tell your strength in one bid; do not turn this into a disadvantage by bidding again without support.

Remember that the jump overcall has definite upper limits. When your hand is too good to make a jump overcall, you probably have the type of hand which should be treated by a double and then a bid of your suit.

You now have all the weapons necessary to describe accurately all types of suit-oriented hands with the exception of highly distributional one- and two-suiters. Notrumps and assorted freaks are next.

Quiz V—The Jump Overcall

With neither side vulnerable, your right-hand opponent deals and opens one heart. What is your bid?

(1) ♠ K J 10 9 8 6	♡ A K	◇ K 6 3	♣ K 4
(2) ♠ 4	♡ A Q 2	◇ A Q J 9 8 3	♣ J 5 4
(3) ♠ A J 9 8 6 3	♡ 4	◇ A 9 2	♣ K 4 3
(4) ♠ 9 8 2	♡ 4	◇ K Q J 9 8 2	♣ K Q 10
(5) ♠ A K Q J 4	♡ 3 2	◇ A J 3	♣ Q 4 3

With only your side vulnerable, what should you, East, do after the following bidding?

SOUTH	WEST	NORTH	EAST
1 ◇	2 ♠	pass	?

(6) ♠ J 3	♡ A J 6 3 2	◇ 7 6 2	♣ K J 3
(7) ♠ 3	♡ J 10 4 3	◇ Q J 4 3	♣ J 9 8 2
(8) ♠ —	♡ K J 5 3 2	◇ Q 5 3	♣ J 5 4 3 2
(9) ♠ 6 3	♡ A K 9 6 3 2	◇ K 5 3	♣ 4 2
(10) ♠ J 4 2	♡ A 7 6 3	◇ 9 7 3	♣ Q 4 2

Answers—Quiz V

(1)	Double	You have too much for a two-spade jump overcall. Double and then bid spades.
(2)	3 ◇	This is a minimum jump to the three level. If you were vulnerable and the opponents were not, you would bid only two diamonds. Without the good secondary cards (9 and 8)

in diamonds, you would bid only two even
with this vulnerability.

(3) 2 ♠   You don't have enough to double and then
              bid spades at the two level.

(4) 2 ◊   This hand is not good enough defensively to
              make a jump overcall.

(5) Double   Double and then bid spades.

(6) 4 ♠   Spades are surely as good as, and probably
              better than, hearts. You may have eight
              hearts; you surely have eight spades.

(7) Pass   Partner's hand is limited. You should be
              able to make two notrump, but if you bid
              two, partner will bid three. And that you
              surely can't make.

(8) Pass   Don't rescue partner from a jump overcall.
              Any new suit you bid is forcing.

(9) 3 ♡   Hearts could be better than spades. If part-
              ner rebids three spades, however, you would
              raise to four.

(10) 3 ♠   This is a standard raise.

8

Notrump Overcalls

♠ ♡ ◇ ♣

The notrump overcall is a strange animal. His personality changes completely according to how high he jumps.

(1) ♠ Q 4   ♡ A J 4   ◇ K J 10 5   ♣ K Q 9 3
(2) ♠ 4   ♡ 6 2   ◇ A J 9 6 3   ♣ K Q J 9 6
(3) ♠ J 3   ♡ K 4   ◇ A 3   ♣ A K Q 10 8 7 3

In each case your right-hand opponent has opened with one heart, and neither side is vulnerable.

You should bid one notrump on hand (1), two notrump on hand (2), and three notrump on hand (3). These are three completely different types of hands; each is described by a different level of notrump overcall. Let's take them one at a time.

THE ONE-NOTRUMP OVERCALL

Bidding one notrump after an opening bid or response describes the equivalent of a one-notrump opening bid. You should have between sixteen and eighteen high-card points and a fairly balanced hand. The one suit which you guarantee to have stopped is the suit which the opener bid. You usually have something in all suits, but you *must* have the opener's suit controlled.

After a notrump overcall the overcalling side proceeds just as if the bidding had been opened with one notrump. If you normally use the Stayman Convention, you would use it. You have learned to open the bidding with one notrump and you have also learned how to respond. The rules you learned also apply to the one-notrump overcall, but here are a few clues which may help and which are relevant to notrump overcalls but not to notrump opening bids.

(1) You need not bid one notrump every time you hold the requirements. There are times when you should stay out of the bidding entirely, because describing your holding may prove too costly. If the bidding comes to you 1 ◇–pass–1 ♠ and you hold

♠ A 3 2   ♡ K J 3   ◇ A 5 4 2   ♣ K J 4

you should not bid at all, regardless of the vulnerability. You have sixteen points and all the suits stopped, but there is an opening bid behind you, and if you get doubled, you will very likely wind up taking only three tricks. You are risking a great deal with nothing to gain. With

♠ K 3   ♡ J 8 2   ◇ Q J 4   ♣ A K Q 10 8

you would still have sixteen points, but you would have a much better notrump overcall. If you get doubled, you will probably be able to take five or six tricks, and the opponents may be missing a game. You have more to gain and less to lose.

(2) When you overcall one notrump over a major-suit opening bid, you tend to deny good support for the other major. You would usually make a takeout double if you held the equivalent of a notrump opening bid but were strong in the other major or majors. Therefore, all the following hands would be one-notrump overcalls after a one-spade opening bid:

(1) ♠ Q J 4 2   ♡ 4 2   ◇ A K J 9   ♣ A Q 4
(2) ♠ A Q   ♡ K 4   ◇ A K 7 3 2   ♣ 6 4 3 2
(3) ♠ K Q 10   ♡ J 6 3   ◇ J 2   ♣ A K Q 4 3
(4) ♠ A J 3   ♡ J 2   ◇ A 4   ♣ K Q J 8 7 3

These hands, however, would be takeout doubles:

(5) ♠ A Q 4	♡ K Q J 3	◇ A 6 3	♣ 10 5 4
(6) ♠ K 4	♡ J 6 3 2	◇ A K 4 3	♣ K Q 4
(7) ♠ A Q 4	♡ K 3	◇ A K 3	♣ Q J 10 4 2
(8) ♠ K 4	♡ K Q 3	◇ A J 4 2	♣ K 10 3 2

Hands (2), (3) and (4) do not appear to fit the usual pattern for notrump, but they are far better notrump overcalls than they are suit overcalls. Even hand (4) works out better with a notrump overcall than with either a jump overcall or a double. With this type of hand you should overcall one notrump even with as little as fifteen high-card points (in this case without the heart jack). If you do overcall with only fifteen, however, you should have either two stoppers in the opponents' suit or a running minor suit.

Hand (5) is very close between a double and a one-notrump overcall. It has been my experience that overcalling one notrump with very good support for the other major works out badly in the long run. You should not want partner to rescue you with a bad five-card major after you overcall one notrump, so don't get him into the habit by having such good support. You tend to deny good support for the other major when you bid one notrump, so if you have a close decision such as this one, decide in favor of a double. With a fourth spade and only a doubleton in one of the minors, you would bid one notrump despite the good heart support.

Hand (7) is too good for a one-notrump overcall. Double and then bid notrump over any response at the two level.

With hands (5), (6) and (8), you would not make another bid over any minimum response by partner. All of these hands lack the playing potential to bid again if partner cannot make a strong reply.

(3)   You should use the Stayman Convention except when the notrump overcall is made over a major-suit opening bid. (As we have seen, the notrump bidder tends to deny the other major. He could, however, have one major when he has bid one notrump over a minor-suit opening bid.)

(4)   There are sixteen-to-eighteen-point hands on which you should pass, not because it is dangerous to bid, but because

you have too much in the suit opened. If your right-hand opponent opened vulnerable with one spade and you held

♠ A Q 10 9 2   ♡ 6 5   ◇ A K 4   ♣ K 5 2

your best action would be to pass. If the hand is passed out, you
will probably score at least two hundred points. If partner has
enough to balance with a double, you will score eight or eleven
hundred. Your left-hand opponent may bid one notrump over
one spade, in which case you would double when it gets back
to you. Partner should leave it in, since you cannot be balancing
in this situation—your hand must be just what it is. On your
really good days your right-hand opponent will bid two spades
over one notrump, and you will double. This again is a penalty
double, since no new suit has been bid by either opponent and
no fit has been found. On your bad days your right-hand opponent will rebid two hearts, and you will have to struggle like
mad to beat it.

With the same hand you should overcall one notrump if
you are vulnerable and the opponents are not. You may have a
notrump game, and you risk too much by passing.

(5) The responder should raise a bit lighter than he
would have if partner had opened the bidding with one notrump.
When the notrump bidder is to the left of an opening bid, the
hand will usually play very well, because all the outstanding
cards are known to be in the opener's hand and the notrump
bidder places his cards over the opener's. Despite the fact that
the opponents will probably be leading their best suit, you can
make many light (23- or 24-point) games.

THE TWO-NOTRUMP OVERCALL: THE INFAMOUS "UNUSUAL NOTRUMP"

Everyone likes a toy, and bridge players are no exception.
The *unusual notrump*—the two-notrump jump overcall and
other notrump bids which show two-suited hands—is the teddy
bear of most bridge players. Actually it is more like a teddy bear
with a firecracker in each paw, considering the reckless use the
average player makes of this device.

Alvin Roth is a genius at the game of bridge. He has added much to bidding theory, and many of the gadgets that top experts employ were developed over the years by Roth and his partners. The unusual notrump is his greatest triumph. In one stroke he gave himself a valuable tool and gave most of his opponents a dangerous device for self-destruction. No single bid in bridge more clearly marks the difference between the expert and the non-expert. Let's try to skip a few years of disasters by learning the basics of these bids and sticking to them.

The most common use of the unusual notrump is the direct bid of two notrump over an opening bid of one. Originally this bid was made only over an opening bid of one of a major or one notrump and showed a hand with two long minor suits. Today most players extend the use to describe a hand with length in the *two lowest unbid suits:* a two-notrump overcall over a one-heart or one-spade bid would mean that the overcaller had long clubs and long diamonds; over a one-diamond bid, it would mean length in clubs and hearts; over a one-club bid, it would mean length in diamonds and hearts. Most players are aware of this meaning, but here their knowledge apparently ends. They seem completely ignorant of the importance of the vulnerability in determining the minimum strength of the suits.

The two following errors lead to most of the disasters in unusual-notrump sequences:

(1)   Bidding every time you hold length in the required suits regardless of the strength of your hand.

(2)   Bidding again after you have already forced partner to name a suit in which he may not be at all interested.

Let's examine the first mistake and see what we can do to avoid making it.

The unusual notrump is used to show either five-five, six-five or six-six distribution in the two lowest unbid suits. It allows you to describe your hand fairly accurately in one bid and at the same time take up a little of the opponents' bidding space. If your suits are of adequate strength, there is not much danger of getting a horrible result, and you will probably wind up either finding a good save or pushing the opponents too high. And what is adequate strength? Adequate strength within one vulnerability situation may be sheer lunacy in another, so in order to play the

unusual notrump with any kind of accuracy, it is necessary that
you learn the following guidelines *and never bid with less.* We
will assume that the opening bid to your right was one heart.

(1)   Not vulnerable vs. vulnerable . . .

     ♠ 5 4   ♡ 5   ◊ K Q 8 7 2   ♣ K J 10 8 2

(2)   Neither side vulnerable . . .

     ♠ 5 4   ♡ 5   ◊ K Q 8 7 2   ♣ A Q 10 8 2

(3)   Both sides vulnerable . . .

     ♠ 5 4   ♡ 5   ◊ A Q 8 7 2   ♣ A Q J 10 2

(4)   Vulnerable vs. not vulnerable . . .

     ♠ 5   ♡ 5   ◊ A Q 8 7 6 2   ♣ A Q J 10 2

When you are not vulnerable and opponents are, you may
use the unusual notrump with a fairly bad hand, because you are
very interested in taking a save for three hundred when the opponents bid a game. As the vulnerability becomes less favorable,
your minimum requirements rise, since you are less interested in
saving and have more to lose if the opponents stop off and
double you at the three level. When vulnerable against non-
vulnerable opponents, you are not at all interested in saving, so
your bid would show a very good hand with game possibilities.
You must also have enough playing strength to avoid a disaster
if partner has no fit and the opponents decide to double you.

Don't use the unusual notrump unless your hand meets the
minimum requirements. If you do, you will not only receive some
large penalties at the three level, but you will also make it impossible for your partner to know when he can afford to save
against a game contract. You will also find yourself committing
error number (2) every time you actually have your bid.

Bidding the unusual notrump without the minimum values
is bad, but raising your partner with minimum hands after a

minimum reply is madness. Consider the following auction with neither side vulnerable:

SOUTH	WEST	NORTH	EAST
1 ♡	2 NT	pass	3 ♣
4 ♡	5 ♣	double	pass
pass	pass		

You are West, and you hold

♠ 5 4   ♡ 5   ◊ K Q 8 7 2   ♣ A Q 10 8 2

With this hand you have contracted to take eleven tricks *without any help from partner*. Remember, you forced partner to choose between the minor suits, so his three-club bid is actually no bid at all, it merely means that he prefers clubs to diamonds. He may, in fact, prefer neither. He may have been dealt:

♠ Q 10 7 6 2   ♡ 8 2   ◊ 9 6 3   ♣ J 4 3

Don't worry though—you don't have to play it, he does.

If you have bid the unusual notrump with minimum values or slightly above minimum values, let partner carry the ball. He knows what you have; you have no idea what he has. If East had held a hand which would make a save profitable such as

♠ A 8 7 3 2   ♡ 6 4 2   ◊ 3   ♣ K J 4 3

he would have bid five clubs over two notrump. He realizes that the opponents probably have a game, and five clubs figures to be a very cheap sacrifice. He may even be able to make it if West has the right cards.

If the two-notrump bidder has a minimum, as he does in the example above, he should not even go to five clubs in the following sequence:

SOUTH	WEST	NORTH	EAST
1 ♡	2 NT	pass	4 ♣
4 ♡	?		

West has described his hand with his two-notrump bid. He
should pass and let East decide what to do. In this case South
may have made a bad move with his four-heart bid, and by passing, West gives his partner the opportunity either to go to game
or to double if he holds something like

♠ A J 2   ♡ Q J 9 7   ◊ 4   ♣ J 7 6 5 4

There are times when the two-notrump bidder can raise
after forcing his partner to pick a suit, but he must hold a hand
which is considerably better than is suggested by his two-notrump bid. If you were not vulnerable and the opponents were,
a raise would be justified in the following auction if you held

♠ 5   ♡ 5   ◊ A Q 8 7 4 2   ♣ K Q 9 8 2

SOUTH	WEST	NORTH	EAST
1 ♠	2 NT	pass	3 ♣
pass	4 ♣		

Considering the vulnerability, you have a very fine two-notrump bid. Four clubs could work out badly, but you may easily
miss a game if you pass. You might even have tried three diamonds to show further interest, but with any other vulnerability
you should pass. You have an exceptional hand only if you are
not vulnerable and opponents are; with any other vulnerability
your hand is only adequate.

What is wrong with the following bidding?

SOUTH	WEST	NORTH	EAST
1 ♡	2 NT	pass	3 ♣
pass	pass	3 ♡	double
pass	4 ♣	double	pass
pass	pass		

What is wrong is that West should have minded his own
business. This is another in the long line of unusual-notrump

disasters. West refuses to let his partner make a decision. He probably has some hand where he shouldn't have bid two notrump in the first place, and he pulls East's double because he thinks they will make it. If East were holding

♠ K Q 4   ♡ Q J 10 9 8   ◊ 4 2   ♣ J 3 2

West would have some explaining to do.

If you have bid the unusual notrump, do not remove any penalty double which your partner makes. These doubles are in no way cooperative. The two-notrump bidder has indicated that he is disinterested in two suits, so if his partner doubles, his partner must have them where he wants them.

It is amazing how well the unusual notrump works when it is handled properly, and how ludicrous it becomes when handled badly. Don't go out of your way to use it with strange partners—especially when calling for suits other than minors.

There are many more subtle uses of the unusual notrump, but we will only go into the most common ones here. Again, they should not be tried with strange partners.

SOUTH	WEST	NORTH	EAST
1 ♡	pass	2 ♡	pass
pass	2 NT		

In this auction West would have something like

♠ 5 4   ♡ 5 4   ◊ A J 10 7 4   ♣ A Q 7 2

He does not want to sell out to two hearts, but he does not know which minor to bid. The unusual notrump in the balancing seat best describes the hand.

SOUTH	WEST	NORTH	EAST
1 ♡	pass	1 NT	pass
2 ♡	pass	pass	2 NT

This auction would suggest somewhat the same hand as the previous sequence, but it is generally not recommended. It is a far more dangerous situation. North and South have not found a fit, and although their hands are limited, there is no reason why you should have any good place to play. Most hands that would qualify for a bid in this situation would have called for an immediate bid of two notrump over one notrump.

More and more partnerships are using opening bids of two spades, two hearts and two diamonds to indicate a good six-card suit and less than an opening bid. Against this treatment—known as the *weak two bid*—you should use a two-notrump overcall to show approximately the equivalent of a notrump opening bid with weakness in the other major or both majors. You would double in much the same way that you would double over opening bids of three.

We have devoted quite a bit of space to the unusual notrump. But it is essential that two general thoughts be kept in mind:

(1)   After bidding two notrump, it is up to you to let your partner make most of the decisions. You will not feel bad about these decisions if you have the values you said you had.

(2)   When your partner bids the unusual notrump, he is expecting you to carry the partnership as far as it can go. Do not simply make a minimum response if you have a good fit for one of partner's suits. Try to picture partner's holding, and if you see that the opponents have a game, try to buy the hand as cheaply as you can in one of partner's suits. Do *not* get enthused about a long suit which partner has denied holding! If you fit one of partner's suits, you have a good hand; if you don't, you have a bad hand.

THE THREE-NOTRUMP OVERCALL

If one notrump over an opening bid shows the equivalent of a notrump opening bid, and two notrump shows a two-suited hand, what does three notrump mean? It means that you would like to try to make three notrump by taking about seven tricks in a minor suit and at least two tricks in outside cards. The bid should have only one meaning—a virtually solid seven-card or longer minor suit with a sure stopper in the opener's suit and at least a partial stopper in one other suit. All of the following hands would qualify as three-notrump bids after a one-heart opening bid:

(1) ♠ 3   ♡ A 4   ◇ A K Q 9 8 6 2   ♣ Q 4 2
(2) ♠ Q 5 3   ♡ K 4   ◇ K   ♣ A K Q J 7 3 2
(3) ♠ A   ♡ K 4   ◇ A K 10 9 7 6 4 2   ♣ J 4
(4) ♠ J 5   ♡ A Q   ◇ K 4   ♣ A Q J 10 6 4 3

There is no guarantee that you can make three notrump on these hands, but even if you can't, the opponents could easily have a game in a suit they have never had a chance to bid. You might even keep them from getting to a heart game. All of these hands are too good for jump overcalls—the seventh card in the suit gives you a bit too much playing strength—and the solidity of your suits makes it unlikely that partner will be able to make a game try. (Partner will never be looking at a good fit, so he will not evaluate his hand very highly.)

It is very important that you bid three notrump over opening one bids only with this type of hand. You should never bid three notrump and turn up with some twenty-five-point square hand. Partnerships must clear up points such as this so that the responder is not put in the position of having to guess what type of hand the three-notrump bidder has. In the 1966 World's Championship, an Italian pair ran into a sequence of one heart— three notrump, and it caused one of the very rare misunderstandings in the long history of the Blue Team's tenure at the top of world bridge. The partner of the three-notrump bidder had about ten high-card points, and he felt that his partner should have a minor-suit hand such as the ones we have described. In fact, the opening bidder had absolutely nothing, and the three-notrump bidder had an evenly distributed twenty five points. Had he made a takeout double, the responder would have made a strong response with his ten points, and a slam would have been reached with ease. Subsequent discussion at the banquet in honor of the again victorious Italians revealed just how differently each of the partners interpreted the bid. The moral is that unless you have the rest of the game worked out as well as the

Blue Team, you should decide now, and remind your partner before playing in the World's Championship, that a three-no-trump overcall over an opening of one of a suit shows a long minor and a good hand.

A bid of three notrump over an opening three bid is not as easy to define. Much of your bidding space has been used up by the three bid, so you may have to bid three notrump with various types of hands.

With neither side vulnerable, the bidding comes to you:

SOUTH	WEST	NORTH	EAST
pass	pass	3 ♠	?

You, East, hold:

(1) ♠ K 4 3   ♡ A 4   ◇ A K Q 6 2   ♣ J 4 3
(2) ♠ A   ♡ 4 2   ◇ J 3 2   ♣ A K Q 10 8 7 3
(3) ♠ A Q   ♡ J 4 2 ◇ A J 9 3   ♣ K Q 4 2
(4) ♠ A 3   ♡ 6 3   ◇ A Q 9 4 2   ♣ A J 6 3

These hands vary greatly, but they are all three-notrump bids. Doubling is out of the question, since you do not have the heart suit—the suit you would be guaranteeing. Overcalling four or five clubs could be right on hand (2), but it is far more likely that you have nine tricks in notrump than eleven tricks in clubs.

Hands (1), (3) and (4)—especially (4)—are a little dangerous, but with South and West both passing originally, it is unlikely that partner has a completely hopeless hand. You will probably be able to keep the three-spade bidder from getting in to run his suit, since he is unlikely to have much outside of spades. Had North been first seat with his three-spade bid, thereby making South's and West's hands unknown quantities, you would have a far greater problem. You would still try three notrump on hands (1) and (2), and possibly on (3), but you would pass hand (4). If you were to get doubled and hurt on hands (1) or (2), at least you would probably be keeping opponents out of a game, but if you were penalized on hands (3) or (4), you would not even have that comfort, since it is unlikely that they would have had game.

Again, you will not always guess right after a preemptive opening bid, but certain bids will work out better than others a good percentage of the time. If bidding three notrump over three spades doesn't turn out right on hand (2), don't stop trying. It is by far your best action.

If your partner bids three notrump over an opening pre-empt—or, more important, an opening one bid—let him play it unless you have a very long, strong major suit to bid. He is probably not interested in hearing about your suit—he may well have a singleton—so don't disturb him with less than Q J 10 8 7 4 and a distributional hand.

Just as you should not always bid one notrump over an opening bid when you apparently have the values, you should be careful about stepping in at three notrump over preempts. It is extremely dangerous to bid three notrump when your partner is a passed hand and the person at your left is not. We discussed the matter of evaluating your hand for bidding over preempts according to who has originally passed and who has not, and these thoughts are just as important here as they were when trying to decide whether or not to make a takeout double. Take some extra time to study and learn the differences in the three following auctions, and you will save yourself quite a few five-hundred-point penalties.

	SOUTH	WEST	NORTH	EAST
(1)	pass	pass	3 ◇	3 NT
(2)			3 ◇	3 NT
(3)		pass	3 ◇	3 NT

East's hand must have better minimum values on each succeeding sequence. In the first case the outstanding cards are likely to be evenly divided, since no one could open the bidding with a one bid. In the second case both South and West have unlimited hands, so you could be running into a big hand to your left. In the third auction partner is known to have less than an opening bid, but your left-hand opponent may be loaded. Common sense dictates that a three-notrump bid in the third case should be made with much stronger minimum values than in the first case.

One more word of advice concerning bidding over preempts: if you believe that you have a close decision between making a takeout double and bidding three notrump, decide in favor of the double if you have good values in the other major or in both majors. Doubles are more flexible than overcalls, and there is always the chance that partner will leave the double in for penalties. It is usually better to pass or bid three notrump with a short holding in the other major; it is usually better to double with a good holding.

♠ A 4   ♡ 6 5 4   ◇ A K J 7 2   ♣ A 6 2

is either a three-notrump bid or a pass over three spades;

♠ A 4   ♡ A 6 5 4   ◇ A K J 7   ♣ 6 5 2

is a double or a pass. If you ask why a double *or* a pass, you should take one more minute to examine the three auctions above.

Quiz VI—Notrump Overcalls

After one pass your right-hand opponent bids one diamond. With both sides vulnerable, what is your best action with these hands?

(1) ♠ 4   ♡ A Q 10 9 6   ◊ 63   ♣ A Q J 8 2
(2) ♠ A 3   ♡ 4   ◊ K 63   ♣ A K Q 9 8 3 2
(3) ♠ K 32   ♡ K 2   ◊ K Q J 4   ♣ Q J 42
(4) ♠ A Q   ♡ 632   ◊ A J 4   ♣ A Q 10 42
(5) ♠ K 3   ♡ A K 63   ◊ K Q 10   ♣ Q 986

Consider the following auction:

SOUTH	WEST	NORTH	EAST
1 ♡	2 NT	double	?

With only the opponents vulnerable, what is your best bid as East?

(6) ♠ K 10 9 8 6   ♡ Q 42   ◊ J 43   ♣ 43
(7) ♠ J 3   ♡ Q 62   ◊ K J 832   ♣ Q 43
(8) ♠ Q J 42   ♡ Q 10 3   ◊ 632   ♣ 842
(9) ♠ 10 532   ♡ J 10 43   ◊ 63   ♣ J 32

SOUTH	WEST	NORTH	EAST
1 ♡	3 NT	double	?

Neither side is vulnerable. What should you do with this East hand?

(10) ♠ A 9 8 6 3   ♡ 42   ◊ J 3   ♣ Q 732

(1) 2 NT   This is a good unusual notrump, asking partner to bid one of the two lower unbid suits.

(2) 3 NT   You have a maximum. All partner needs is some sort of heart stopper.

(3) Pass   This is a very dangerous hand. The opponents very likely can't make a game, but you might easily get hurt if you bid. If you hold the opponents' suit and lack the values for a one-notrump overcall, it is usually best to pass.

(4) 1 NT   You have no heart stopper, but you have a good hand, and one notrump is more descriptive than a double. Two clubs is out!

(5) 1 NT   This is a perfect one-notrump overcall. By playing the Stayman Convention, you will be able to find your heart fit if your partner has a game-going hand.

(6) 3 ◊   Partner is asking you to bid a minor, so do so unless your spades are very strong and long. North's double probably means he has a good hand, but you shouldn't be hurt too badly in three diamonds.

(7) 5 ◊   The opponents have a major-suit game. Bid five diamonds right away and let them guess what to do.

(8) Pass   Let partner choose his best suit.

(9) 3 ♣   This is like no bid at all. You merely prefer playing clubs to diamonds. Partner should not bid again unless he has six-six.

(10)   Redouble   Don't give partner the chance to run out. You have all the right cards to make three notrump, but partner will not know it if you pass. You should not even consider bidding four spades.

9

Preemptive Overcalls

♠ ♡ ◇ ♣

Any jump overcall in a suit which skips more than one level describes a one-suited hand and is preemptive. These bids begin one level higher than an intermediate jump overcall. 1 ♣–2 ◇ would show a good hand, but 1 ♣–3 ◇, or 1 ♣–4 ◇, or 1 ♣–5 ◇ would all show very distributional hands, with the strength depending very largely on the vulnerability.

For the most part, preemptive overcalls correspond closely to opening three, four, and five bids, so that only when vulnerable, and especially vulnerable against non-vulnerable opponents, should you have any great strength. The primary purpose of such a bid is to take up as much of the opponents' bidding room as is possible with reasonable safety. It is extremely important that you not use any preemptive jump, *including jumps to game*, when you hold a very strong hand, with the exception of a jump to game when vulnerable against non-vulnerable opponents. (With this vulnerability, you must have a hand which can take at least eight tricks, or else you would be risking an eight-hundred-point penalty against a non-vulnerable game.)

Just as an opening three, four or five bid changes with the vulnerability, so do all levels of preemptive overcalls. A hand such as

♠ 3 2   ♡ A Q J 10 8 7 2   ◇ 8 7 5 2   ♣ —

on which you would bid three hearts over one club if neither side were vulnerable, would be worth a four-heart bid if only the opponents were vulnerable. With

♠ 5　　♡ 5 4　　◇ A K J 8 7 6 4 2　　♣ 3 2

you would bid five diamonds over an opening one bid if only the opponents were vulnerable, four diamonds if the vulnerability were equal, or nothing at all if you were the only ones vulnerable. (Had the opening bid been one club, you might try three diamonds with the last vulnerability.)

There are two good reasons why you shouldn't have a big hand when you jump to game.

(1)　You will not know what to do if the opponents bid again.

(2)　Partner will not know what to do if the opponents bid again.

SOUTH	WEST	NORTH	EAST
1 ♣	4 ♡	4 ♠	?

With only North and South vulnerable, you are East and hold:

♠ J 4　　♡ 10 9 8 2　　◇ 8 7 6 5 4　　♣ 6 2

Pass! Partner *guarantees* a bad hand with a long, strong heart suit. The opponents are a cinch to make either six or seven, and if you bid, you will induce South to support spades. If you pass, South may decide to pass too, because he does not know if North has a big hand or just a hand with which he does not want to be shut out of the bidding. In an auction such as this, North's hand has a very wide range of possibilities. As far as South knows, he could have as little as

♠ A Q 9 8 4 3　　♡ 3　　◇ J 9 3 2　　♣ 5 4

or as much as

♠ A K 10 7 6 2　　♡ 3　　◇ A Q 3 2　　♣ J 3

You know that he has the latter type of hand, but South doesn't.

If you bid five hearts, South will give a competitive raise, and North will go to six; on the other hand, if you pass, South will probably pass.

Too bad—you were playing with an undisciplined partner who decided to bid four hearts with a good hand, which is a horrible tactic with this vulnerability. He holds:

♠ A K   ♡ A Q J 7 6 5 3   ◊ 2   ♣ 7 5 4

They make four spades, while you should have bid and made five hearts. Competitive bidding is a partnership affair, so don't go out of your way to destroy your rapport. Had your partner doubled one club and then jumped in hearts, you would have gone to the five level.

Both sides are vulnerable; your right-hand opponent deals and bids one club. What is your action with the following hands?

(1) ♠ Q J 10 9 8 3 2   ♡ A 5 4   ◊ 6 3   ♣ 4
(2) ♠ 4   ♡ K Q J 9 8 7 6 2   ◊ A 5 3   ♣ 2
(3) ♠ A K J 8 6 2   ♡ A 6 3   ◊ 2   ♣ Q 4 2
(4) ♠ 6 3   ♡ K Q J 10 9 6 3   ◊ 6 3   ♣ 6 3

Hand (1) is a fine three-spade bid. You have a good suit, little defensive strength, no outside major suit and enough playing strength to take six or seven tricks.

Bid four hearts on hand (2). You can take eight tricks, and a four-heart bid may keep them from finding a spade game if they have one. You might even make four hearts.

Hand (3) is a perfect two-spade bid. You have the exact values for an intermediate jump overcall.

Pass hand (4). It is tempting to bid three hearts, but 7–2–2–2 distribution is not a good preempting distribution. With a singleton somewhere, you would have a minimum three-heart bid with this vulnerability.

RESPONSIBILITIES OF THE RESPONDER

It is important that the responder understand what to do when partner makes a preemptive jump. There is almost no holding that justifies rescuing partner if he gets doubled in a preemptive overcall. You would only rescue if you can do so at the same level, and if you have a terrific seven-card suit of your own.

Any time partner makes a preemptive jump, he is taking a risk. He may have stuck his nose in at the wrong time, and the result could be a five-hundred-point penalty against nothing. It is essential, then, that you offset these disasters by getting the most out of the times when he is right. You must be alert to further the preempt when it is correct to do so, stay out of the action when further bids are futile and punish the opponents when they have been pushed way overboard. Most important, it is essential that you recognize when the opponents are in their worst possible contract and not disturb them.

With the opponents vulnerable, the bidding comes to you:

SOUTH	WEST	NORTH	EAST
1 ♣	4 ◊	4 ♠	?

What should you do with the following holdings?

(1) ♠ Q 4 3   ♡ J 5 3 2   ◊ J 4 3   ♣ A 6 2
(2) ♠ J 4 3   ♡ J 6 5 3 2   ◊ J 4 3   ♣ 6 2
(3) ♠ K Q 10   ♡ A 5 3 2   ◊ 4   ♣ Q 10 9 8 2
(4) ♠ A Q 10 8 3   ♡ J 4 3   ◊ 6 2   ♣ J 4 3

Bid five diamonds on hand (1). Partner is showing either an eight-card suit or a seven-card suit with better playing values than needed for a three-diamond bid. You might beat them if they bid again, and if they double you, it shouldn't be expensive.

Pass hand (2). This is a futile situation. If you bid, you increase the chances of getting them to slam.

Double with hand (3). There is some chance that they can make four spades, but if North was stretching to bid four spades, they could go down two or three. More important, they have no better place to go.

You should not dream of doubling hand (4). Four spades is the only contract which you have any chance of beating, and if you double, you will be giving North a chance to show his club support. If they leave in four spades doubled, you may not even beat it. Declarer will play all the other suits, and you will wind up having to lead spades. It appears that North has been put in a bad position by the preempt. He probably holds something like

♠ K J 9 7 2   ♡ A 7 2   ◊ 5   ♣ Q 9 6 2

He wanted to bid both four spades and five clubs. If you double, you give him the chance.

Don't expect any defensive tricks when partner makes a preemptive jump—especially when not vulnerable against vulnerable. This does not mean that you can't double with hands like number (3); it simply means that you must be careful not to make loose doubles on the strength of partner's bid. His bid is actually showing minus values, so don't make close doubles which give away the location of the trump suit or which give the opponents another chance to find their best spot. Partner's preempt has taken away much of their bidding space—don't give it back to them by doubling.

If partner has made a preemptive jump and your right-hand opponent bids three notrump, you must be very careful about doubling with less than three cards in partner's suit. You will have to take all the tricks yourself, since partner almost surely has no entry.

What all this amounts to is that you should not punish partner for having preempted. He has made the opponents guess at a high level. Unless you are reasonably sure that they have guessed wrong *and* that they have nowhere to go, don't double.

RULE NUMBER 1 FOR THE PREEMPTER

We will conclude this chapter with a sound word for the preempter: *having once preempted, do not rebid your suit.*

SOUTH	WEST	NORTH	EAST
1 ♣	4 ◊	4 ♠	pass
pass	?		

Bidding again in this sequence is *impossible*. There is no excuse for a five-diamond bid. Partner has heard your four-diamond bid and decided to let the opponents play four spades. He may be afraid that five diamonds will be too expensive. Or he may think he can beat four spades but nothing else. Or he may be afraid that a further bid will get the opponents to six. *Do not bid again.*

Quiz VII—Preemptive Overcalls

With only the opponents vulnerable, your right-hand opponent deals and opens one diamond. What is your best action with the following hands?

(1) ♠ 6   ♡ 8 6 3   ◇ 9 2   ♣ K Q J 8 7 6 2
(2) ♠ A J 10 8 7 3 2   ♡ 4   ◇ 9 8 6 ♣ 5 2
(3) ♠ 4   ♡ A K J 9 8 6 3 ◇ 8   ♣ 8 6 3 2
(4) ♠ A Q J 10 8 7 6 ♡ A K   ◇ 4   ♣ K 3 2
(5) ♠ 4   ♡ 4 2   ◇ K 4   ♣ K Q J 10 9 8 6 3

SOUTH	WEST	NORTH	EAST
1 ♣	3 ♡	double	?

With neither side vulnerable, what should you do with these hands?

(6) ♠ K Q 8 7 6 2   ♡ 4   ◇ A 4 3 2   ♣ 4 2
(7) ♠ Q J 10 9 7 6 3   ♡ 4   ◇ Q 6 3 2   ♣ 4

SOUTH	WEST	NORTH	EAST
1 ♣	4 ♡	4 ♠	?

Only the opponents are vulnerable. What would you, East, do with the following hands?

(8) ♠ 6 4 3 2   ♡ K 6 2   ◇ A 9 6 3   ♣ 4 2
(9) ♠ K Q J 4   ♡ 6 5 2   ◇ 6 5 2   ♣ Q 4 3
(10) ♠ K J 9 8   ♡ 5 4   ◇ A 4 3   ♣ Q 9 8 3

(1) Pass   Three clubs would show a good hand, and four clubs is a bit excessive. Two clubs is possible, but you should usually have a bit more high-card strength for any two-level overcall.

(2) 3 ♠   With this vulnerability you have a perfect three-level preemptive overcall.

(3) 4 ♡   With 7–4–1–1 distribution and a good suit, four hearts isn't too much.

(4) Double   You will bid four spades next, thereby showing a good hand.

(5) 5 ♣   Make it as tough as possible.

(6) Pass   Partner has a better suit than you do, and he probably is short in spades. You have one and possibly two tricks for him; he may have none for you.

(7) 3 ♠   You have no tricks for partner, and you should be able to take at least as many tricks as he can.

(8) 5 ♡   You should have a good save, and you may be able to beat them if they bid again.

(9) Pass   You may be able to beat four spades, but you may not be able to beat anything else. Partner denies defense with his four-heart bid.

(10) Double   It appears that the opponents have reached too high a level.

10

The Direct Cue-Bid

♠ ♡ ◇ ♣

You have already been introduced to the cue-bid. It is used both after a takeout double and after an overcall, but in this chapter we will limit our discussion to one of the original uses of the cue-bid—the direct cue-bid of the opener's suit.

If you cue-bid the opener's suit directly, or if you cue-bid the responder's suit without an intervening bid from partner, you are describing a hand which is the equivalent of a strong opening two bid. Partner can't pass until a game is reached.

On many hands where you would make a direct cue-bid, you could just as easily make a takeout double and then cue-bid, but there are other hands where a takeout double is unattractive because you have a very distributional hand with either one or two suits. A cue-bid comes in handy with these hands because partner has no chance to pass, as he does with a takeout double.

Your right-hand opponent opens one heart. What would you do with the following hands?

(1) ♠ A K J 10 4   ♡ 3   ◇ 3   ♣ A K Q 9 7 3
(2) ♠ A K   ♡ — ◇ A K J 9 8 7 2 ♣ A J 10 4
(3) ♠ A K Q J 9 8 7 2 ♡ 3 ◇ A K   ♣ 3 2

All of these hands are best treated with direct cue-bids. You want to be in game somewhere, and you do not want partner to pass one heart doubled. Bid two hearts and then:

Hand (1): If the opponents stay out of your way, you will bid clubs and then spades. Partner cannot pass until game is reached. If the opponents interfere, you may not be able to bid both suits. Try four spades and hope your partner has three small ones.

Hand (2): This hand appears to be a diamond hand, but if partner insists on spades or notrump, you should let him play. He may have a six-card spade suit and a singleton diamond. Game is not guaranteed on this hand, but bidding anything but two hearts would be extremely cowardly. Problems might arise if your left-hand opponent bids four hearts and partner bids four spades. You would be forced to guess, but five diamonds seems logical.

Hand (3): Jump to four spades. You should, however, cue-bid first, so partner will know you have a good hand. Jumping to four spades immediately makes further competitive bidding guesswork.

It is very unlikely that you will have many opportunities to use the direct cue-bid in this form. You don't hold too many game hands after an opening bid. Do not further limit the use of the bid by insisting, as some players do, that the cue-bid promises no losers in the cue-bid suit.

Most experts have given up using the direct cue-bid to show enormous hands. There are all sorts of different meanings that have been attached to this bid, the idea being to get more use out of the call. In a future book in this series the more recent uses of the direct cue-bid, as well as many other specialized expert conventions, will be discussed in detail. Do not worry for the present that you are missing out on the answers to all your bidding problems. Most beginning players spend an unnecessary length of time in utter confusion because they insist on trying to learn and play every new convention that is dreamed up. I strongly suggest that you keep your bidding as simple as possible until you feel that you have a very firm knowledge of the basics. Only then will you be able to make any kind of intelligent decision about which of the modern gadgets are right for your game.

Good Luck!

Quiz VIII—Direct Cue-Bids

SOUTH	WEST	NORTH	EAST
1 ◇	?		

The opponents are vulnerable. Some of the following hands are better doubles than cue-bids. Some are better cue-bids. Which ones are which, and why?

(1)	♠ A K J 8 7	♡ A K 4	◇ 3	♣ A Q J 3
(2)	♠ A Q J 10 9	♡ A Q 10 8 7 3	◇ 4	♣ A
(3)	♠ A	♡ A K J 10 8 7 3	◇ K 4	♣ A Q 4
(4)	♠ A J 10	♡ A Q 4 3	◇ A 4	♣ K J 10 4

SOUTH	WEST	NORTH	EAST
3 ◇	4 ◇	5 ◇	?

What should you do if you are vulnerable and the opponents are not?

(5)	♠ J 4 3 2	♡ A 10 5 3 2	◇ 6 4 3	♣ 2
(6)	♠ 5 3 2	♡ 7 6 2	◇ J 3 2	♣ 10 4 3 2
(7)	♠ 6 5	♡ K J 8 4 2	◇ 6 3 2	♣ 8 7 3
(8)	♠ K 7 6 2	♡ A 5 3 2	◇ 9 8 7	♣ 6 3

Answers—Quiz VIII

(1)	Double	If partner wants to leave the double in, you would be delighted. (The opponents are vulnerable.) If he bids a suit, you will cue-bid and then select the best game contract.

(2)   2 ◇   Your object is to get to the better major-suit game or slam. You may have to repeat the cue-bid in order to get partner to bid his better major.

(3)   2 ◇   After partner bids, you will jump to four hearts. This bidding shows a better hand than either a direct jump to four hearts (pre-emptive) or a double followed by a jump to game.

(4)   Double   This may not even be a game-going hand.

(5)   Pass   In a situation where the opponents are obviously saving, a pass shows an interest in partner's going on. This principle is called the *forcing pass,* and it is a very common occurrence. In this case partner has shown a terrific hand, and you would like to play five of a major. A pass lets him decide what to do. He may have a hand with long spades and short hearts, in which case a five-heart bid by you would be disastrous.

(6)   Double   You don't want to go further, and a double tells partner that you would like to take a profit against five diamonds. If you pass in a situation where the opponents are obviously saving, you ask partner to bid something if he wishes.

(7)   5 ♡   You have a decided preference for hearts.

(8)   6 ◇   With an ace, a king and four cards in each major, you want partner to bid six of his better major. You might even have tried six diamonds on hand (5).

Index

Index

Aggressive action after doubles, 56

Balancing doubles, 14, 17-23, 79-80
  responses to, 54
Balancing overcalls, 79-81
  suit evaluation for, 79

Cue-bids
  defined, 5
  direct, 143-44
  as responses to one-level overcalls, 39, 99-101
  as responses to three-level doubles, 49
  as responses to takeout doubles, 42-46
  rebids by doubler as, 59
  to show interest in majors, 49

Defensive bidding, basic goals of, 1
Delayed takeout doubles, 12-15
  responses to, 53-54
Doubles
  after both opponents have bid, responses to, 53-54
  four- and five-level, responses to, 52-53
  after overcalls, 102-3
  penalty, 11, 14-17, 55

takeout, see Takeout doubles
three-level, responses to, 48-51

Forcing pass, defined, 146

High card requirements
  for one-notrump overcalls, 117
  for responses to takeout doubles, 37-39
  for three-notrump overcalls, 126-27

Intermediate jump overcalls, 109-10

Jump overcalls, 109-14
  defined, 4
  intermediate, 109-10
  weak, 109
Jump raises
  after one-level overcall, 87-89
  in rebidding by doubler, 57-58
  as responses to takeout doubles, 38-39, 46-48

Leads
  indicated by overcalls, 69
  after partner passes your takeout double, 63

Mathe, Lew, 85

Notrump
  bidding, when vulnerable, 96
  rebidding, after minimum re-
    sponse by partner, 60-61
  as response to one-level overcall,
    96-98
Notrump overcalls, 117-30
  one-notrump, 117-20
  two-notrump ("unusual"), 120-
    26
  three-notrump, 126-30

One-notrump opening bid doubled,
    15
One-notrump overcall, 117-20
  responses to, 117-18
One-notrump response to takeout
    doubles, 40-41
Opening bids, doubles of, 7-9
  of one-notrump, 15
Overbids, as British term for over-
    calls, 3
Overcalls, 69-81
  balancing, 79-81
    suit evaluation for, 79
  defined, 3-4
  at high levels, 77-78
  jump, 109-14
    defined, 4
    intermediate, 109-10
    weak, 109
  limiting factors for, 70
  minimum values for, 70-72
  objectives of, 69, 85, 103-4
  one-level, 70-75, 86-101
    bidding new suit after, 93-96
    bidding notrump after, 96-97
    cue-bidding after, 98-101
    raising partner's suits after,
      86-92
    when to pass after, 90-91
  one-notrump, 117-20
    responses to, 117-18
  preemptive, 135-40
    defined, 4
    responses to, 137-40

three-notrump, 77, 126-30
  defined, 4
two-level, 75-76
  responses to, 101-2
unusual notrump, 120-26
  defined, 4
when doubled after, 102-3
when vulnerable, 70
  high-level situations, 77-78
  jump overcalls, 111-12
  one-level overcalls, 75
  preemptive overcalls, 135-36
  three-notrump overcalls, 128
  two-level overcalls, 76

Pass, forcing, defined, 146
Penalty doubles, 11, 14-17, 55
Preemptive bids, takeout doubles of,
    21-23
  responding to, 48-53
Preemptive overcalls, 135-40
  defined, 4
  responses to, 137-40

Raises
  jump
    after one-level overcalls, 87-89
    in rebidding by doubler, 57-58
    as responses to takeout dou-
      bles, 38-39, 46-48
  of partner's suit after one-level
    overcall, 87-93
Rebidding
  by doubler
    after minimum response, 56-
      61
    after stronger response, 62-63
  after preemptive overcall, 139-40
Redoubles, responder's action after,
    54-55

Saves
  defined, 13
  by overcalls, 69, 78, 81

Saves (cont'd.)
  by takeout doubles, 13-14
Suit requirements
  in balancing overcalls, 79-80
  in one-level overcalls, 70-75
  for one-notrump overcalls, 117
  in overcall objectives, 69
  with rebids by doubler, 58
  for response to one-level over-
    call, 93-96
  for response to takeout double,
    8-9, 29

Takeout doubles, 7-27
  after both opponents have bid,
    10-12
  balancing, 14, 17-23, 79-80
    responding to, 54
  delayed, 12-15
    responding to, 53-54
  direct double at one level, 7-9
  general tips for, 63-64
  at higher levels, 15-17
  after original pass, 10
  overcalling compared to, 77
  penalty doubles and, 11, 14-17
  of preemptive bids, 21-23
    responding to, 48-53
  rebidding by doubler after, 56-63
  responses to, 29-64
    direct, 31-40
    cue-bid, 42-46
    high card requirements, 37-39
    jumps, 38-39, 46-48
    one-notrump, 40-41
    responder's action after redou-
      ble, 54-55

suit requirements, 29
two- and three-notrump, 41-42
when to bid, 29-30
when to pass, 30
setting up saves, 13-14
Three-notrump overcalls, 77, 126-
    30
  defined, 4
Three-notrump responses
  to takeout doubles, 41-42
  to three-level doubles, 51
Trumps as leads, 63
Two-notrump overcalls (unusual
    notrump), 120-26
  defined, 4
Two-notrump response to takeout
    doubles, 41-42

Unusual notrump, 120-26
  defined, 4

Vulnerable
  bidding notrump when, 96
  overcalls when, 70
    high-level situations, 77-78
    jump overcalls, 111-12
    one-level overcalls, 75
    preemptive overcalls, 135-36
    three-notrump overcalls, 128
    two-level overcalls, 76

Weak jump overcall, 109

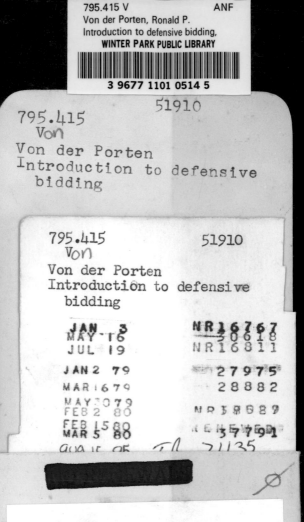